Christ Community Chapel
Hudson Campus- Library
750 W Streetsboro Street
Hudson, OH 44236
(330) 650-9533 ext 112

COMING HOME

Other Gospel Coalition Books

Don't Call It a Comeback: The Old Faith for a New Day, edited by Kevin DeYoung

Entrusted with the Gospel: Pastoral Expositions of 2 Timothy, edited by D. A. Carson

God's Love Compels Us: Taking the Gospel to the World, edited by D. A. Carson and Kathleen B. Nielson

God's Word, Our Story: Learning from the Book of Nehemiah, edited by D. A. Carson and Kathleen B. Nielson

The Gospel as Center: Renewing Our Faith and Reforming Our Ministry Practices, edited by D. A. Carson and Timothy Keller

Gospel-Centered Youth Ministry: A Practical Guide, edited by Cameron Cole and Jon Nielson

Here Is Our God: God's Revelation of Himself in Scripture, edited by Kathleen B. Nielson and D. A. Carson

His Mission: Jesus in the Gospel of Luke, edited by D. A. Carson and Kathleen B. Nielson

The Pastor as Scholar and the Scholar as Pastor: Reflections on Life and Ministry, by John Piper and D. A. Carson, edited by David Mathis and Owen Strachan

The Scriptures Testify about Me: Jesus and the Gospel in the Old Testament, edited by D. A. Carson

Seasons of Waiting: Walking by Faith When Dreams Are Delayed, by Betsy Childs Howard

Word-Filled Women's Ministry: Loving and Serving the Church, edited by Gloria Furman and Kathleen B. Nielson

The Gospel Coalition Booklet Series
Edited by D. A. Carson and Timothy Keller

Baptism and the Lord's Supper, by Thabiti M. Anyabwile and J. Ligon Duncan III

Can We Know the Truth?, by Richard D. Phillips

Christ's Redemption, by Sandy Willson

The Church: God's New People, by Timothy Savage

Creation, by Andrew M. Davis

The Gospel and Scripture: How to Read the Bible, by Mike Bullmore

Gospel-Centered Ministry, by D. A. Carson and Timothy Keller

The Holy Spirit, by Kevin L. DeYoung

Justification, by Philip Graham Ryken

The Kingdom of God, by Stephen T. Um

The Plan, by Colin S. Smith

The Restoration of All Things, by Sam Storms

Sin and the Fall, by Reddit Andrews III

What Is the Gospel?, by Bryan Chapell

COMING HOME

Essays on the
New Heaven and New Earth

EDITED BY

D. A. CARSON
and
JEFF ROBINSON SR.

WHEATON, ILLINOIS

Coming Home: Essays on the New Heaven and New Earth
Copyright © 2017 by the Gospel Coalition
Published by Crossway
      1300 Crescent Street
      Wheaton, Illinois 60187

First printing 2017

Printed in the United States of America

Unless otherwise indicated, Scripture quotations are from the ESV® Bible (The Holy Bible, English Standard Version®), copyright © 2001 by Crossway, a publishing ministry of Good News Publishers. Used by permission. All rights reserved.

Trade paperback ISBN: 978-1-4335-5397-4
ePub ISBN: 978-1-4335-5400-1
PDF ISBN: 978-1-4335-5398-1
Mobipocket ISBN: 978-1-4335-5399-8

Library of Congress Cataloging-in-Publication Data
Names: Carson, D. A., editor.
Title: Coming home: essays on the new heaven and new earth / edited by D. A. Carson and Jeff
    Robinson Sr.
Description: Wheaton: Crossway, 2017. | Series: The gospel coalition | Includes bibliographical
    references and index.
Identifiers: LCCN 2016040231 (print) | LCCN 2017001776 (ebook) | ISBN 9781433553974 (tp) | ISBN
    9781433553981 (pdf) | ISBN 9781433553998 (mobi) | ISBN 9781433554001 (epub)
Subjects: LCSH: Redemption—Biblical teaching.
Classification: LCC BT775 .C66 2017 (print) | LCC BT775 (ebook) | DDC 234/.3—dc23
LC record available at https://lccn.loc.gov/2016040231

Crossway is a publishing ministry of Good News Publishers.

CH	27	26	25	24	23	22	21	20	19	18	17
15	14	13	12	11	10	9	8	7	6	5	4	3	2	1

*To the members of
the council of the Gospel Coalition
whose Christ-centeredness and love provide
an intimation of the glory yet to come*

CONTENTS

PREFACE

Diff eschatological perspectives

The manner in which Christians have thought about life after death, or about the world to come, has varied considerably from century to century and from place to place. It is easy enough to understand why. Christians who have few of this world's goods or who face the stress of perennially threatening persecution are more likely to long for the "home" of the new heaven and the new earth than are Christians who live remarkably secure and comfortable lives. Christians who think about these things at a period in history when talk about "end times" is all the rage are more likely to stretch their imaginations into eternity (though how accurately is another question) than are those who focus on other doctrines. And Christians who faithfully read their Bibles right through, again and again, will inevitably be drawn to ponder the return of Jesus more faithfully and more fruitfully than will those who rarely take pains to hide God's Word in their hearts.

Among the grand themes uncovered by focused Bible reading are these five (and this list is representative, not exhaustive):

First, Jesus teaches that our hearts pursue what we treasure (Matt. 6:21). So if we are to pursue the supreme good of knowing and seeing God in the new heaven and the new earth, we will have *to treasure* it as the supreme good. This is more than a confessional point of the sort that says, "I believe in the reality of the new heaven and the new earth, and in the life everlasting." Rather, that supreme good must be *treasured*, for that is what will make our hearts pursue it. Otherwise we will devote all our energy to pursuing lesser things, things that may in many cases be good, but that are squeezing out the supreme good precisely because the supreme good is not treasured. That means that one of the goals of the preacher must be so to disclose and promote the supreme good that Christians hungrily pursue it.

Second, although Christians have good reasons to believe that when they die they enjoy disembodied existence in the presence of Christ, their ultimate hope is not death, not what has traditionally been called "the intermediate state." Rather, it is the return of Christ, the dawning of the new heaven and the new earth, which is the home of righteous, embodied existence—resurrection existence.

Third, Christians who are hungry to understand their Bibles are eager to discover how various important trajectories "work" in Scripture. In other words, how do we run from the garden of Eden to the new heaven and the new earth? Where do themes like justice, priesthood, life, Trinity, incarnation, justification, sanctification, resurrection, temple, grace, covenant, people of God, and much more, fit into the patterned mosaic that takes us to Revelation 21–22?

Fourth, a variety of biblical depictions of the new heaven and the new earth insist, in colorful terms, that neither sin nor sin's entailments are there: there is no greed, no hate, no lust, no death, no sorrow, no tears. Conversely, we will love God with heart and soul and mind and strength, and our neighbors as ourselves. There will be no more struggle for justice, for all of us will be just before God, and practitioners of justice in every way. So what are the relationships between the sinless state of Eden and the sinless existence of the new heaven and the new earth? The storyline of the entire Bible turns on how human beings, made in the image of God, fell into sin and were graciously redeemed by the God who made them. What does that tell us about the significance of our struggle against sin now?

Fifth, that storyline turns on Jesus the Messiah. The gospel is first and foremost the good news of what God has done through his Son, supremely in his death and resurrection, to redeem his chosen and blood-bought people back to himself. Those who enjoy the new heaven and the new earth join the choir around the One who sits on the throne, *and the Lamb*. It is impossible to think richly and faithfully about eschatology without thinking richly and faithfully about Jesus Christ; it is impossible to focus on him without reflecting on eschatology.

The eight chapters of this book expound select passages from the Old and New Testaments that deal with these themes. They are the written forms of eight plenary addresses of the 2015 national conference of the Gospel Coalition. Our hope is that circulating them in this form will help many more people revel in the richness of God's Word—not only of these discrete passages but also of some of the ways these passages unfold the developing lines of Scripture and call our minds and imaginations home to the new heaven and the new earth. The final plenary session of the conference, preserved as an appendix in this book, preserves the probing and sometimes moving panel discussion titled "Biblical Foundations for Seeing God's Justice in a Sinful World." And in the end, we face the call of God for more than mere justice—the call of God to respond with the grace of the gospel.

It is a great privilege to work with those whose conference voices are preserved in these pages. Thanks, too, to Jeff Robinson, who undertook the initial editing of these chapters, and to the visionary folk at Crossway, who live out what it means to seek the kingdom of God and his righteousness.

D. A. Carson
Soli Deo gloria

1

LIFE AND PROSPERITY, DEATH AND DESTRUCTION

Deuteronomy 30:1–20

TIMOTHY KELLER

Deuteronomy 30, which comes at the end of Moses's life, describes how Moses hands off Israel to new leaders. The people have entered into a covenant relationship with God at Mount Sinai, where God in essence said, "I will be your God, and you will be my people. This is how I want you to live. Here are the stipulations of the covenant."

Now that Moses is about to pass off the scene, the Israelites are renewing the covenant, and Moses writes Deuteronomy as a documentation of that covenant renewal. All the things that the children of Israel are supposed to do in order to live as the people of God are laid out. It's a wonderful exposition of the Ten Commandments and of what it means to lead lives of integrity and justice. Near the end of the covenant renewal document, in Deuteronomy 27–28, God through Moses lays out what is referred to twice in Deuteronomy 30:1–20 as "blessings and curses."[1] God in

---

1. Unless otherwise indicated in the text, Scripture references in this chapter are taken from The Holy Bible, New International Version®, NIV®. Copyright © 1973, 1978, 1984, 2011 by Biblica, Inc.™ Used by permission. All rights reserved worldwide.

effect says, "If you obey the covenant and are faithful to what you say you are going to do for me, I will bless you." The beginning of chapter 28 is filled with all the ways in which God will bless the people for obedience. But then, in the last three-quarters of chapter 28, God essentially says, "If you disobey the covenant, all these terrible curses will come upon you," as he said above in 30:18, "I declare to you this day that you will certainly be destroyed" if you disobey the covenant. The curses will come upon you.

These curses are truly ferocious, and yet the blessings are equally astounding. The blessings always come along with the promise that God is gracious, that he is forgiving, and that he overlooks sin. Since the blessings are so gracious and seemingly so unconditional, and the curses are so ferocious and so obviously conditional (*"If* you do this, you will be destroyed"), many scholars believe Deuteronomy was written by more than one person. In their *Introduction to the Old Testament,* Raymond Dillard and Tremper Longman III cite one of the classic Old Testament professors, F. M. Cross, as having read the book of Deuteronomy and concluded as much.

Cross believed that Deuteronomy was written in two stages, with the first probably at the time of King Josiah, when there was a lot of hope. On this assumption, the first copy of Deuteronomy would have contained these gracious promises of blessing, where God was portrayed as a gracious, forgiving, and faithful God who overlooks sin and pardons iniquity. But then, Cross claimed, after the disaster of the Babylonian exile, the Israelites found Deuteronomy too optimistic and somebody else wrote another edition of the book and added all the curses. Cross could not believe that any one person could have held together both these amazing blessings and these horrific curses, and therefore no one person could have written Deuteronomy. In fact, Cross could not even fathom a God who could be both so gracious and so deadly, so loving and so holy.

Dillard and Longman do a wonderful job of completely destroying that idea. They're almost comical about it, as if to say, "Can you imagine an editor so incredibly incompetent that he takes a document that's too optimistic about God's love, adds these verses on holiness, judgment, and justice, and then also leaves in everything he disagreed with in the first place, so that it's just a mishmash of contradictions?" Frankly, that would be a pretty stupid editor.[2]

Tension between His Mercy and Holiness

Although Cross was wrong in that point, he saw rightly the tension displayed in Deuteronomy's blessings and curses. The book of Deuteronomy, possibly for the first time in the biblical narrative, makes it extremely clear that there is such a tension, and we humans brought it about. We have a holy God of justice who must punish sin and who cannot clear the guilty. He basically says to Moses in Exodus 34, "I can't let any sin go unpunished!" Yet at the same time, he is a God of endless love, endless faithfulness, and endless forgiveness, and he desires a relationship with us. But because of our flawed and sinful nature, there is an unresolved tension at this point in Deuteronomy. One might ask, How can God be both faithful to who he is in terms of his mercy, and faithful to who he is in terms of his holiness?

David Martyn Lloyd-Jones addressed this tension in one of his sermons on revival. He pointed out that in Exodus 33, Moses asks to see God's glory and God replies, "'I will cause all my goodness to pass in front of you, and I will proclaim my name, the LORD, in your presence. I will have mercy on whom I will have mercy, and I will have compassion on whom I will have compassion. But,' he said, 'you cannot see my face, for no one may see me and live'" (Ex. 33:19–20). Just a few verses later God comes down, Moses is shielded, and

---

2. See Tremper Longman III and Raymond B. Dillard, *An Introduction to the Old Testament*, rev. ed. (Grand Rapids, MI: Zondervan, 2006), chap. 6.

he [God] passed in front of Moses, proclaiming, "The LORD, the LORD, the compassionate and gracious God, slow to anger, abounding in love and faithfulness, maintaining love to thousands, and forgiving wickedness, rebellion and sin. Yet he does not leave the guilty unpunished; he punishes the children and their children for the sin of the parents to the third and fourth generation." (Ex. 34:6–7)

Lloyd-Jones explains the apparent contradiction. God says his "goodness" will pass in front of Moses, and when this happens, the first thing he says is, basically, "I am forgiving, and yet every sin has to be punished." While this may seem like a paradox, Lloyd-Jones answers by posing the question Why is it that God must punish every sin? God must punish every sin because he is so good! If a judge saw that somebody committed a crime and said, "Oh well, let it go," then he wouldn't be a good judge. Likewise, the reason why God must punish every sin is that he's so good.

On the other hand, why would God want to forgive us, love us, and never let us go? You guessed it—because he's so good. "But," you say, "how in the world can there be a God who is that comprehensively good?" He must either be fully good in terms of his holiness and justice but not in terms of his love (meaning you better obey, because his patience is short and only obedience will get you into heaven), or be fully good in terms of his love but not in terms of his holiness and justice (meaning God would say, "Well, I'd *like* you to obey, but in the end I'll accept you no matter what you do"). But either way, there's no God who is completely and comprehensively good. Having it both ways seems impossible. As we saw earlier, that's exactly what F. M. Cross and many other Old Testament scholars believed. When they read Deuteronomy and saw the blessings and curses, they concluded that there's no God who could be both so gracious and so ferocious. Instead, they claimed Deuteronomy must be the product of two editors, one with a more benign view of God and a second with a more ferocious view.

But contrary to what those scholars believed, the Old Testament purposefully has an unresolved narrative tension in it, and this very tension is the whole basis of the gospel. Narrative tension means you don't know what's going to happen and there are opposing forces at work. In other words, "Little Red Riding Hood took her grandmother some goodies" is not a narrative. It's just a report. "Little Red Riding Hood took her grandmother some goodies, but the Big Bad Wolf was waiting to eat her up" is a narrative, because we've got tension. We're led to ask, What's going to happen? The narrative tension that drives the whole book of Deuteronomy is the same narrative tension that drives the whole narrative arc of the Bible, all the way up to the cross.

"But," you reply, "I guess it doesn't get resolved in Deuteronomy." Yes and no. What is beautiful about the Bible is the wonderful foreshadowing we see throughout it of how the resolution is going to happen, and there is foreshadowing here in Deuteronomy 30.

Deuteronomy 30 and the Future

Deuteronomy 30 says much about the future, and although in one place it looks like Moses is speaking about the present, we will see how Paul explains in Romans 10 that Moses is still talking about the future. Let's look at three things Moses says.

First, in the future, we will all fail to live as we ought. Second, God will fix our hearts. Third, the message of the gospel will go out.

You Cannot Be Good

The first thing Deuteronomy says about the future is that we will all fail to live as we ought. This is one of the most important things about Deuteronomy 30. In fact, if you don't keep this in mind, you'll misread the last part of the chapter. Look at verse 1: "When all these blessings and curses I have set before you come on you and you take them to heart wherever the LORD your God disperses you among the nations . . ." Moses says that the Israelites will be dispersed. If you go back into Deuteronomy 28, where you see a list of terrible curses, the ultimate curse is exile and dispersion. And so verse 1 is essentially saying, "You will fail. You will bring all the curses of the covenant down on you. The worst that God says will happen to you if you disobey the covenant will in fact happen."

American readers of Deuteronomy will know how our culture loves motivational speakers. We enjoy having people tell us what we can do and how we can live. In some ways, the whole book of Deuteronomy is like a motivational speech. It's a wonderful ethical treatise. It's a vision for integrity, justice, and human life at the highest. Moses is preaching the first sermon series in history, as some have described Deuteronomy, and he's basically saying, "I want you to live like this," much as a motivational speaker would speak today.

But how does Moses's motivational speech end? After he tells the Israelites to live according to the ethical standards of Deuteronomy 1–29, he effectively concludes, "Let me point this out. You're going to fail! You're not going to do any of this stuff I'm talking about! You're going to fail miserably! I am wasting my breath!"

You might say that's not good motivational speaking, and you'd be right. But it is great gospel preaching. Of course, that's not all there is to gospel preaching (praise God!), but unless you're willing to affirm this, you're not able to do any gospel preaching. What is Moses saying? He looks at the Israelites, who here represent the whole human race, and he pretty much says, "You know what you ought to do. This isn't rocket science. If there is a God, you owe him this: love your neighbor as yourself, and love God with all your heart, soul, strength, and mind. You know what you should do, but you're not going to do it."

Jacob Needleman has been a secular philosopher and a professor of philosophy of religion for many years at San Francisco State

University. Some years ago he wrote a remarkable book called *Why Can't We Be Good?* His thesis is that even though social theorists, therapists, politicians, and everybody else are working like crazy to write books about how people should live, there's just one thing they're forgetting: everybody basically knows how he or she ought to live, and we just can't do it. Nobody's got the strength to do what we know we should. This, says Needleman, is the biggest mystery and problem of the human race. Why are we writing all these books telling people how they ought to live? People know what they ought to do, but they just won't and can't do it. It's impossible. And people know they should *not* do certain things, but they do them anyway. That's our problem, Needleman says. Human beings know how they should live but they can't and they won't, and he has no idea why.

There's a great story related to this problem in Rebecca Pippert's book *Hope Has Its Reasons*.[3] Pippert writes of when she once audited a class in counseling psychology at Harvard University; the professor gave a case study of a man who was very angry at his mother. The man didn't realize how angry he was, so his anger was distorting his life. Through counseling, this man came to see how much his life was being dominated by his anger, and that seemed to help. But as the professor was moving on to another case study, Pippert raised her hand and asked, "Well, that's great, but how do you help the person?"

"What do you mean?" replied the professor.

"Well, how do you help him forgive his mother?" Pippert asked. "If his life is being distorted by his resentment toward his mother, how do you help him forgive his mother?"

The professor's first response was basically to say, "There isn't anything I can do. Hopefully now he will understand his anger and hopefully not be as driven by it." Most of the other students in the class were a little surprised and discontented with this answer,

---

3. Rebecca Manley Pippert, *Hope Has Its Reasons: The Search to Satisfy Our Deepest Longings*, rev. ed. (Downers Grove, IL: InterVarsity, 2001).

so the professor concluded the discussion by saying nearly the same thing as Needleman: "If you guys are looking for a changed heart, you are looking in the wrong department."

As the professor had to admit, psychology can't help you do what you ought to do. Even if it can show us what to do, we don't do it. We *can't* do it. For this reason, I often have used Francis Schaeffer's illustration to explain Romans 2 whenever I have spoken to an unbelieving audience. Romans 2 says the Gentiles—the pagans who don't know the law of God and don't know the Bible—still have in their conscience a certain knowledge of how they should live, and God holds them responsible for what the conscience tells them. Schaeffer used to tell the following story to prove this point.

Imagine you have an invisible recorder around your neck that, for all your life, records every time you say to somebody else, "You ought." It only turns on when you tell somebody else how to live. In other words, it only records your own moral standards as you seek to impose them on other people. It records nothing except what you believe is right or wrong. And what if God, on judgment day, stands in front of people and says, "You never heard about Jesus Christ and you never read the Bible, but I'm a fair-minded God. Let me show you what I'm going to use to judge you." Then he takes that invisible recorder from around your neck and says, "I'm going to judge you by your own moral standards." And God plays the recording.

There's not a person on the face of the earth who will be able to pass that test. I've used that illustration for years now and nobody ever wants to challenge it. Nobody ever says, "I live according to my standards!" This is the biggest problem of the human race. We don't need more books telling people how to live; people need the power to do what they don't have the power to do.

Just as Moses begins by telling the Israelites, "You're going to fail," gospel preachers have to constantly remind people what they already know in their hearts but won't admit: "You know what to do, and you never will do it unless you get some kind of outside help. You will never pull yourself together."

GOD FIXES HEARTS

But the second thing Deuteronomy says about the future is that God has a plan to fix hearts. In Deuteronomy 30:2–5, Moses predicts that the Israelites will be put into exile and that God will bring them back. But when Moses gets to verse 6, he says, "The LORD your God will circumcise your hearts and the hearts of your descendants, so that you may love him with all your heart and with all your soul, and live." He's talking about something that the rest of the Bible brings out. Jeremiah and Ezekiel call it the new covenant. Paul in Romans 2:29 says that our hearts are circumcised, and in Philippians 3:3 he says we are the true circumcision. So this is the gospel, and this is looking far beyond anything that actually happens in the lives of the Israelites at that time.

And what is a circumcised heart? As frequently noted by many expositors, "heart" in English means the seat of the emotions, but "heart" in the Bible means the control center of the whole being. Proverbs 3:5 says, "Trust in the LORD with all your heart," because that's what hearts do. Genesis 6:5 speaks of the "inclination . . . of the human heart" because that's what hearts do. In Matthew 6:21, Jesus says "For where your treasure is, there your heart will be also." Your heart is the place where you decide what you're going to trust, take inclination to, and treasure; it's where you decide what your supreme good is, what your ultimate hope is, and what you're going to think about all day.

A good test of this is seen in the much-cited saying "Your religion is what you do with your solitude." Think about that. What is it that your heart most cherishes, most adores, most trusts in, and most hopes in? What is the thing you most look to for your salvation? What is the thing your mind automatically goes to when you have nothing else to think about? That may be hard for us to imagine because social media and cell phones have made solitude hard to obtain, but at my age, I can remember a time when I would stand waiting for a bus with nothing to do and nothing to think about. I never took those five minutes to praise God or think about his glories, his attributes, and what he'd done for me. My heart tended to fantasize about other things, like "If only the church could get to this number, then maybe we could build a wing."

What do you think about at the bus stop? The heart is the indicator of what you love most. Whatever the heart most wants, that is the thing that the mind finds reasonable, the emotions find desirable, and the will finds doable. In other words, what the heart is set upon affects your mind, your will, and your emotions.

Now that we've examined what Scripture means by "heart," what does it mean to have a "circumcised" heart? It sounds like a scary idea, doesn't it? Peter Craigie, in his commentary on the book of Deuteronomy, says that when Deuteronomy speaks of God circumcising the heart, it's a metaphor (strange though it may be) for God doing surgery on your heart. It could also be said that whereas circumcision was a sign of external obedience, entry into the covenantal community, and submission to the law of God, heart circumcision is the motivation of inner love to obey. In fact the text says, "The LORD your God will circumcise your hearts and the hearts of your descendants, so that you may love him with all your heart and with all your soul, and live" (Deut. 30:6).

To use another metaphor, think about marriage. Over the years there have been many political and business marriages where the proverbial knot was tied, but there was no love. But when I was falling in love with my wife, and she asked me to make a change in my life—the sort of thing that my mother or father used to ask me to do and I would say, "Mind your own business"—Kathy's wish was my command. I was in love, so I didn't think of it as obeying her or submitting to her will, though in a sense I was. She wasn't demanding anything, but out of love I was changing that thing in my life.

That's what it's like to have a circumcised heart: what you ought to do and what you want to do become the same thing. Or as John Newton said in one of his hymns,

Our pleasure and our duty,
Though opposite before,
Since we have seen his beauty,
Are join'd to part no more.[4]

Our pleasure and our duty are the same. That's a circumcised heart.

If you grew up attending church, you probably heard the word *circumcision* in Sunday school. Of course, when you were little, you asked a lot of questions. But when you asked, "What is circumcision?" nobody ever told you what it means! It wasn't until you were older that the topic came up again, and you were taught that circumcision was the sign that someone had entered into a covenant relationship with God. Once the teacher explained circumcision, if you were like most people, you said, "You're kidding! Why in the world would God ask anyone to do that? What was that about?"

Yes, circumcision was gross and bloody, but that was the point. In the days of the Old Testament, you didn't just sign a paper contract when you wanted to make a covenant. Instead, you acted out the curses of failing to keep that covenant. You would cut an animal in half, walk between the pieces, and say something like "Oh great king, the one to whom I make my vow today, if I do not do all the words of the promise which I am making today, may I be cut to pieces like this animal." That's how you would act out the curse of not keeping the covenant. In my opinion, that was a lot better way of doing contracts than we have today. People would be more likely to follow through on promises that way!

If you understand the way people made covenants in that era,

---

4. John Newton, "Shall Men Pretend to Pleasure."

then you begin to see what circumcision represents. Circumcision is gory, bloody, gross, and intimate; it's downright creepy! Why not some other part of the body? Why not something less disturbing? It's a way of showing people the penalty of sin. Sin is so dire, so intimate, and so gross, it could only be represented by something like circumcision. So why do we still talk about the circumcised heart?

There's a strange phrase in Colossians 2:11 that could be literally translated, "In Christ, you [Christians] have been circumcised in the circumcision of Christ." Paul is teaching that you receive not only a new heart when you become a Christian, but a circumcised heart because of the circumcision of Christ. And what is the circumcision of Christ? On the cross, Jesus Christ was experiencing the curse of the covenant: to be cut off. If you lie, cheat, or wrong someone else, being cut off from the congregation is the penalty that Deuteronomy gives again and again. But the penalty for disobeying God is to be cut off from him. To be cut off from God is to be cut off from life, light, and every good thing. On the cross, Jesus was suffering that penalty. He was suffering the cosmic experience that we deserve, the punishment for our sin.

Think back to the garden of Eden. Adam and Eve were forced out—or cut off—because of their sin, and an angel with a sword was stationed to guard the way to the tree of life. The only way back to the tree of life was to go under the sword, and on the cross, Jesus Christ went under the sword. In that sense, he was circumcised.

Because Jesus Christ experienced that circumcision for you and me, when we put our faith in him, not only do we objectively have a relationship with him, but subjectively that image of Christ suffering the curse for us on the cross makes our pleasure and our duty the same. As quoted before, John Newton said it best:

> Our pleasure and our duty,
> Though opposite before,

Since we have seen his beauty,
Are join'd to part no more.

And what is that beauty of which Newton speaks? In the words of William Cowper:

To see the Law by Christ fulfilled
And hear His pardoning voice,
Changes a slave into a child,
And duty into choice.[5]

If seeing what Jesus Christ did on the cross for you—taking your cosmic "cutting off" for you—moves you and you say to yourself, "I do deserve to be cut off and Jesus did that for me," then you know you're experiencing the circumcision of the heart.

JESUS HAS DONE THAT FOR YOU

The third and final thing Deuteronomy says about the future comes at the end of the passage, where we noted earlier that it seems to speak only about the present. So far, Deuteronomy 30:1–6 has been looking down the corridors of time, saying in effect, "First, you're going to fail, all the curses are going to come upon you, and you will go into exile, but then God will bring you back and circumcise your heart." That's the promise of the new covenant and the new birth. But then Deuteronomy 30:11–15 reads:

Now what I am commanding you today is not too difficult for you or beyond your reach. It is not up in heaven, so that you have to ask, "Who will ascend into heaven to get it and proclaim it to us so we may obey it?" Nor is it beyond the sea, so that you have to ask, "Who will cross the sea to get it and proclaim it to us so we may obey it?" No, the word is very near you; it is in your mouth and in your heart so you may obey it.

See, I set before you today life and prosperity, death and destruction.

---

5. William Cowper, "Love Constraining to Obedience," 1772.

It may seem like Moses is coming back to the present when he describes what he is commanding the Israelites "today." He says his law is not too difficult but is very near to them, even in their mouth and heart. What does that mean? On the one hand, it means that the Israelites have no excuse. The law of God is very clear. They don't have to go over the sea to talk to sages or to mystics to figure out what God's will is; instead, it's come to them. "'Love the Lord your God with all your heart and with all your soul and with all your strength and with all your mind'; and, 'Love your neighbor as yourself'" (Luke 10:27). The law is laid out plainly, so they have no excuse. And yet, as Thomas Schreiner points out in his commentary on Romans,[6] Paul would later quote this passage in Romans 10 knowing that Moses has already said that the Israelites cannot and will not keep this covenant. Therefore, Paul is absolutely right in interpreting what Moses means when the apostle says in Romans 10:4, 6–9:

> For Christ is the end of the law for righteousness to everyone who believes.
>
> . . . But the righteousness based on faith says, "Do not say in your heart, 'Who will ascend into heaven?'" (that is, to bring Christ down) "or 'Who will descend into the abyss?'" (that is, to bring Christ up from the dead). But what does it say? "The word is near you, in your mouth and in your heart" (that is, the word of faith that we proclaim); because, if you confess with your mouth that Jesus is Lord and believe in your heart that God raised him from the dead, you will be saved. (ESV)

Schreiner says Paul is applying Moses's words to show that in the end the only word that will not crush you, that is not too difficult for you, and that you don't have to go over the sea to get is the gospel. Jesus has already done the impossible for you. Don't try to earn your salvation, Paul says. To do that is to bring Jesus up

---

6. Thomas R. Schreiner, *Romans*, Baker Exegetical Commentary on the New Testament (Grand Rapids, MI: Baker, 1998).

from the abyss or keep Jesus back in heaven. He came from heaven and went into the abyss to save you. If you try to save yourself, it's like telling Jesus that what he did doesn't matter. Only the gospel is the word that is not too difficult for you, and only the gospel will not crush you. Any other word will. Therefore, Moses is basically saying, "Someday the gospel will go forth."

Heaven and Hell Are Not Parallel

Without a doubt, the blessings and the curses point forward to heaven and hell. But did you notice they're not parallel? In other words, if you go to hell, it's your fault. You deserve it. Deuteronomy 30 makes that clear. But if you get the blessings of God, there's no way you deserve that. That has been accomplished and given to you freely. We must never give anybody the impression that hell is deserved *and* heaven is deserved. Hell is deserved, and heaven is not.

You can see it clearly in the way blessings and curses are discussed in Deuteronomy. The prosperity gospel says they're equal: if you do this, you'll be blessed, but if you do that, you'll be cursed. But as Christopher Wright notes in his commentary on Deuteronomy,[7] if you do wrong, you deserve the cursing. If you do right, that only appropriates the blessing; it doesn't deserve it. Obedience is simply a way for you to appropriate the blessing that Jesus Christ has deserved for you. That difference is very clear in the book of Deuteronomy and must be maintained as we think about the afterlife and in all of our preaching on it.

---

7. Christopher J. H. Wright, *Deuteronomy* (Peabody, MA: Hendrickson, 1996).

2

THE SHOOT FROM JESSE, THE NATIONS, AND ISRAEL

Isaiah 11

JOHN PIPER

The book of Isaiah begins, "The vision of Isaiah the son of Amoz, which he saw concerning Judah and Jerusalem in the days of Uzziah, Jotham, Ahaz, and Hezekiah, kings of Judah" (1:1). So the prophecies of Isaiah are mainly concerning the southern kingdom of Judah from about 740 to 700 BC. Looming on the horizon is the massive empire to the east, Assyria, huffing and puffing with threats against Jerusalem.

Isaiah hears Assyria in 10:13 boasting,

By the strength of my hand I have done it.
. . . .
like a bull I bring down those who sit on thrones.

But God has already made clear in 10:5 that this huffing and puffing Assyria is a mere tool in his hand: "Woe to Assyria, the rod of my anger." So when Assyria boasts that it has cut down the great, God says in 10:15, "Shall the axe boast over him who hews with it?" And when God has done his work with this tool, Isaiah says in 10:12, "he will punish the speech of the arrogant heart of the king of Assyria and the boastful look in his eyes."

Then the word of judgment on Assyria comes to climax in 10:33–34:

> Behold, the Lord GOD of hosts
>   will lop the boughs with terrifying power;
> the great in height will be hewn down,
>   and the lofty will be brought low.
> He will cut down the thickets of the forest with an axe,
>   and Lebanon will fall by the Majestic One.

So with a picture in front of us of a vast forest of nothing but jagged stumps that God has made by hewing down the power of Assyria, Isaiah prophesies the coming of the Messiah as a shoot from the stump of Jesse (11:1):

> There shall come forth a shoot from the stump of Jesse,
>   and a branch from his roots shall bear fruit.

Jesse was the father of King David. So we know that Isaiah is prophesying the fulfillment of 2 Samuel 7, that a son of David—a new shoot of Jesse—will come and rule the people of Israel and rule the world. All of Isaiah 11 is a description of that Son of David—that shoot, that branch—and the kingdom he will rule.

And what is so typical of the prophets, and so mystifying to us, is that chapter 10 flows into chapter 11 seamlessly, as if chapter 10 would happen on Monday and chapter 11 would happen on Tuesday. Read it again without the chapter division:

> [God] will cut down the thickets of the forest with an axe,
>   and Lebanon will fall by the Majestic One.
> There shall come forth a shoot from the stump of Jesse.
>   (10:34–11:1)

Not the slightest indication that there might be seven hundred years or twenty-seven hundred years separating these events.

Prophetic Perspective

When I was cutting my teeth on the prophetic books in seminary, one of the really helpful things I was taught was that the
way prophets looked at the future was the way we may look at a
mountain range with distant mountains and nearer mountains in
the one mountain range, all of them looking like one mountain.
For example, to the north of our home in Pasadena was Mount
Wilson. From where we stood on East Orange Grove Boulevard,
it looked like one mountain. But in fact, if you started hiking, or
driving, you quickly found that it was not merely one mountain,
but a series of ever-higher ridges with valleys in between, about
five of them.

We called that the "prophetic perspective." From where Isaiah
stood, God granted him to see the Mount Wilson of the future.
Some of the nearer ridges of Sennacherib's comings and goings
he knew were very near, and when they would happen (e.g., Isa.
37:29). But beyond that there were other events he saw on Mount
Wilson with no clear idea about how distant they were. So repeat-
edly in the prophetic books you read of an imminent attack by or
deliverance from an enemy, and the next moment you read about
an event in the distant future, with no indication of how much
time is in between.

The apostle Peter says in 1 Peter 1:10–11, "Concerning this
salvation, the prophets who prophesied about the grace that was
to be yours searched and inquired carefully, inquiring what person or time the Spirit of Christ in them was indicating when he
predicted the sufferings of Christ and the subsequent glories." In
other words, when the Spirit moved the prophets to write, he did
not answer all their questions about how the pieces fit together.
Which means that as we read the prophets, not all our questions
may be answered either.

However, we do have some advantages over the prophets—
which may sound strange, since they were inspired by God, and
we are not. First, we have *all* the prophets, so we can compare

them with each other, and we have the New Testament use of the prophecies; and second, we have the perspective of twenty-seven hundred years to see what has happened. So, strange as it may sound, we may understand the timing and the relationships of some things more clearly than they did.

Avoiding Overreactions to Prophecy

This leads me to insert an exhortation and prophecy of my own here. Many evangelicals in my generation have held dispensational eschatological charts in such derision that they have been virtually paralyzed in their study of prophecy. For two generations, perhaps, we have failed to study prophecy with anything like the rigor that it deserves. We have been so afraid of being viewed as one of those Zionist, right-wing, Antichrist sniffing, culture-denying, alarmist leftovers from the Scofield/prophecy-conference era that we give hardly any energy to putting the prophetic pieces together—at least not in public.

So my prophecy is that younger evangelicals who take the Bible seriously will start to feel like the paralysis of my generation was an overreaction to prophetic studies; Chris Tomlin and others will write more worship songs about the second coming; and younger scholars will not be embarrassed to write doctrinal dissertations on Daniel 9 and Matthew 24 and 2 Thessalonians 2, unintimidated by the academic scorn of futuristic possibilities.

And my exhortation is this: Go for it! But in the process don't lose any of the real gains of the last sixty years—like the chastening of our abilities to predict the end, and the full-blooded engagement with the challenges of this present day. If anything is clear from the prophets, it is that their prophecies were meant to empower present, God-centered righteousness and sacrifice for the relief of all suffering and, we know now, especially of eternal suffering.

So as we walk through Isaiah 11, we will not be able to avoid some of these prophetic perplexities and controversies. But, oh, the riches that are here, and that are clear!

Four Parts

Chapter 11 has four parts, as I see it. First, verses 1–5 describe the Son of David and the way he rules his kingdom. Second, verses 6–9 describe the peace of that global kingdom where the knowledge of God fills the earth and the wolf lies down with the lamb (11:6). Third, in verse 10, the nations of the world come to the Messiah and find rest in his glory. And fourth, in verses 11–16, the remnant of Israel gathers from the four corners of the earth (11:12).

PART 1: THE CHARACTER OF THE SHOOT OF JESSE,
THE SON OF DAVID, AND HOW HE RULES (ISA. 11:1–5)
Isaiah 11:1–2 says:

> There shall come forth a shoot from the stump of Jesse,
>   and a branch from his roots shall bear fruit.
> And the Spirit of the LORD shall rest upon him.

This is very similar to Isaiah 61, which Jesus applied to himself in Luke 4:18, "The Spirit of the Lord is upon me." And so Jesus saw himself as the fulfillment of this prophecy. He was the shoot from the stump of Jesse.

Isaiah 11:2 continues:

> The Spirit of wisdom and understanding,
> the Spirit of counsel and might,
> the Spirit of knowledge and the fear of the LORD.

Wisdom and understanding are the foundation for being able to give good counsel and rule well with might. And the aim of all counsel and power is to know the Lord and to fear the Lord, and to fill the earth with the knowledge and the fear of the Lord. So the shoot of Jesse has everything he needs to bring God's world back from its rebellion to the knowledge of God and the fear of the Lord.

In verse 3 we read, "And his delight shall be in the fear of the

LORD." What a statement! It is so contrary to the emotions of the world. His joy is to stand in awe of God. His joy is to tremble at the terrible prospect of displeasing God. This makes him utterly reliable in his judgments among men. Isaiah continues:

> He shall not judge by what his eyes see,
>> or decide disputes by what his ears hear,
> but with righteousness he shall judge the poor,
>> and decide with equity for the meek of the earth;
> and he shall strike the earth with the rod of his mouth,
>> and with the breath of his lips he shall kill the wicked.
> Righteousness shall be the belt of his waist,
>> and faithfulness the belt of his loins. (11:3b–5)

His judgments are not based on the appearance or the opinions of others. His joy is in the fear of the Lord, not the fear of man.

So his rule will be just. The righteous oppressed will be vindicated, and the wicked will be killed. Paul uses these final words of verse 4 ("with the breath of his lips he shall kill the wicked") in 2 Thessalonians 2:8, where he says, "Then the lawless one will be revealed, whom the Lord Jesus will kill with the breath of his mouth." That's a reference to the second coming of Christ. Which means that Isaiah 11:1–5 includes descriptions of Jesus in his first coming and his second coming with no hint of any time lapse. This is a Mount Wilson glimpse of King Jesus as he is in his first coming and as he is in his second coming, viewed as one great mountain range of Christ's rule. Only subsequent events and further revelation reveal how it works out.

PART 2: THE PEACE OF CHRIST'S GLOBAL KINGDOM (ISA. 11:6–9)

Isaiah 11:6–9 offers this picture:

> The wolf shall dwell with the lamb,
>> and the leopard shall lie down with the young goat,
> and the calf and the lion and the fattened calf together;
>> and a little child shall lead them.

The cow and the bear shall graze;
> their young shall lie down together;
> and the lion shall eat straw like the ox.
The nursing child shall play over the hole of the cobra,
> and the weaned child shall put his hand on the adder's den.
They shall not hurt or destroy
> in all my holy mountain;
for the earth shall be full of the knowledge of the LORD
> as the waters cover the sea.

It is a picture of something radically new. The summary of the point is given in verse 9, first negatively, then positively:

They shall not hurt or destroy
> in all my holy mountain.

Hurting forces and destructive forces that touch animals and children will be gone. How? Amazingly, Isaiah gives this reason (and it really is a ground clause in Hebrew) in verse 9b:

for [*because*] the earth shall be full of the knowledge of
> the LORD
> as the waters cover the sea.

So Isaiah depicts a global kingdom. And in it is an earthly kingdom with animals. And the animals will behave according to the knowledge of God. Where the earth is filled with the knowledge of God and that knowledge is no longer suppressed (as in Rom. 1:18), changes even in nature are profound and pervasive. The spirit of the King—the spirit of knowledge and the fear of the Lord—is so present and powerful that it fills the earth with the knowledge of God and changes everything.

When will this happen? In Isaiah 65:25 the earlier prophecy is repeated almost exactly:

The wolf and the lamb shall graze together;
. . . .

They shall not hurt or destroy
    in all my holy mountain,
        says the LORD. (cf. Isa. 11:9)

And that is the climax of a paragraph in Isaiah 65 that begins,

Behold, I create new heavens
    and a new earth,
and the former things shall not be remembered
    or come into mind. (65:17)

So we are reading a description of the new heavens and the new earth when we read of the wolf and the lamb grazing together and the child playing on the hole of the cobra.

But there's a glitch in the timing. In the middle of that description of the new heavens and the new earth in Isaiah 65:17–25, verse 20 says that the child who plays with the cobra, unharmed, grows up and dies in ripe old age.

No more shall there be in it [in the Jerusalem of the new earth]
    an infant who lives but a few days,
    or an old man who does not fill out his days,
for *the young man shall die a hundred years old*,
    and the sinner a hundred years old shall be accursed.

So here we have the new earth described as a place where animals don't kill each other, and where children don't die in infancy. Instead they live a long life, full of the knowledge of the Lord, and then at least some of them die in very old age. And mingled with them are sinners who also live long lives and then are cursed (65:20).

What are we to make of this? Is it a new earth with death and sin in it? One solution (the most common solution of amillennialism) is to say that these words are metaphorical; the reference really is to the final state where there is no death and no sin. Another solution (the solution of premillennialism) is to say that this is another higher ridge in the mountain range of redemptive history where the wolf and the lamb will lie together, infant mortality will be overcome, but death and sin will not yet be completely removed.

I have read again the efforts of the best expositors I know to explain how a young man dying at a hundred years old is an effective metaphor for people never dying. I haven't been able to see it. One of the best scholars on Isaiah says, "What we have no capacity to understand can be grasped only through what we know. . . . We are dealing with metaphor." The problem with this is that we do have a capacity to understand what it would mean if Isaiah said, "A young man will never die." That is *not* beyond our capacity to understand. And I am not helped to grasp the perfectly clear idea that death will be no more by the so-called metaphor that says, "The young man shall die a hundred years old." That doesn't seem to me like an effective metaphor of never dying.

So my suggestion is that when Isaiah 65:17 says, literally, "Behold, I am creating [בּוֹרֵא, qal participle] new heavens / and a new earth," he means God is creating it in stages. Its newness does not appear all at once. The first coming of the Messiah opens the first stage of the final redemption. The second coming of the Messiah opens another stage described in Isaiah 65:17–25, and at the end of that period, the final state of sinless, deathless perfection in creation will come.

To be fair, it might be true to say that historic premillennialists like me sometimes use fanciful speculations about how to make the conditions in the millennium work, and amillennialists sometimes use fanciful exegesis to make texts show there is no millennium after the second coming. This is why, among other reasons, the Gospel Coalition does not include millennial views in its founding and defining documents—a decision that I think was a very good one. While we may not all agree how many mountain ridges there are on the way to the top of Mount Wilson, we are thrilled to agree that when the history of redemption is done, there will be no death, there will be no sin, the lion will lie down with the lamb in the new earth, and Jesus will be King.

PART 3: THE NATIONS OF THE WORLD COME TO THE MESSIAH AND FIND REST IN HIS GLORY (ISA. 11:10)

Isaiah 11:10 says, "In that day the root of Jesse, who shall stand as a signal for the peoples—of him shall the nations inquire, and his resting place shall be glorious [literally *glory*]." Paul quotes this verse in Romans 15:12 as something that is coming true in his own mission to the Gentiles.

God means for the nations of the world to be part of the kingdom of the Messiah. The root of Jesse is a signal to all the nations of the world: Come, seek the Messiah. His rest is glory. He will welcome you. Join him.

PART 4: THE GATHERING OF THE REMNANT OF ISRAEL FROM THE FOUR CORNERS OF THE EARTH (ISA. 11:11–16)

I won't deal with Isaiah 11:11–16 verse by verse, but notice the focus on the remnant of Israel scattered among the nations. Verse 11 says, "In that day the Lord will extend his hand yet a second time to recover the remnant that remains of his people." The second time probably refers back to the exodus, since that's referenced in verse 16 and because the word for "recover" is used (in Ex. 15:16) to describe how God purchased Israel at the exodus.

Isaiah 11:12 continues,

He will raise a signal for the nations
    and will assemble the banished of Israel,
and gather the dispersed of Judah
    from the four corners of the earth.

Not only are the nations to come to the signal of the Messiah, but they should rejoice in the return of Israel and provide no obstacle. Oh how I would love to talk with you about how this relates to

Romans 11, but alas, we have already bitten off more than we can chew.

Then Isaiah 11:15–16 tells us that the Lord will make a way from Egypt and from Assyria, the two greatest powers—to illustrate that no earthly power will hinder the final purposes for the world.

I close with three applications.

Three Applications

Jesus, the shoot from the stump of Jesse, is God's saving signal to the nations today. Lift it up. Isaiah 11:10 says, "In that day the root of Jesse, who shall stand as a signal for the peoples—of him shall the nations inquire." When Paul gives an account of his calling to the nations where Christ is not named, he says in Romans 15:8–9, "Christ [the Messiah] became a servant to the circumcised . . . in order that the Gentiles might glorify God for his mercy." And then he quotes (among other passages) Isaiah 11:10 from the Septuagint:

> The root of Jesse will come,
>   even he who arises to rule the Gentiles;
> in him will the Gentiles hope. (Rom. 15:12)

This is the central meaning of our time. Christ reigns to reach the nations.

The twentieth century was the century of the greatest expansion of the Christian church in the history of the world. While Europe and Canada and Australia experienced dramatic losses through secularization, South America, Africa, and Asia exploded in unprecedented ways. Whether the United States will follow the other Western powers into the irrelevance of total secularization and fall away from God's great purpose for the nations, I don't know. God owes us nothing.

But this I do know, that while the church in America has any strength at all, we should pour ourselves out for the nations—the unreached peoples of the world. We are in the days of a great prophetic fulfillment. The signal of the shoot of Jesse—Jesus Christ, crucified and risen—is being lifted up among the nations, and they are streaming to the Savior of the world. I pray that you will be among those who with their last ounce of energy will lift up the signal for the nations (Isa. 11:10).

The shoot of Jesse judges with truth and calls his people to be a people of righteousness and truth. Isaiah 11:3–4 says that the shoot of Jesse

> shall not judge by what his eyes see,
>
> . . . .
>
> but with righteousness he shall judge.

Jesus uses these words in John 7:24: "Do not judge by appearances, but judge with right judgment." In other words, Jesus takes a prophecy spoken about the kind of person *he* would be and applies it the kind of persons *we* should be. Paul does the same kind of thing in Ephesians 6:14. The belt of right judgment that the shoot of Jesse wears in Isaiah 11:5 becomes the belt of truth that we should wear.

God is calling us, by the shoot of Jesse, to be people of radical truthfulness and righteousness. We do not judge by appearances. Racial differences do not make a person guilty or innocent. High standing in the corporate world or wearing a police uniform does not privilege a person before the law.

The shoot of Jesse calls us to be people of unimpeachable integrity—people of truth. He calls us to be people who go the extra mile in all our dealings and all our promotions and advertising to avoid giving any misleading impressions whatsoever. He is calling us to be a people who put our names on what we have written. And what others have helped us write, their names should go on it too. We do not follow the dishonest ways of the world to make a buck or save a soul.

And we will get our facts right before we make judgments about other people. We will be slow to trust our first condemning impressions. We will write to people and call them and ask if these things are so. We will follow the shoot of Jesse.

> He shall not judge by what his eyes see,
>   or decide disputes by what his ears hear,
> but with righteousness he shall judge. (Isa. 11:3–4)

We will do this because he *is* the truth, and we are the people of truth. The belt of truth holds everything together.

And how was the root of Jesse so free from the craven need for human approval that he didn't care about human appearances or rumors? Isaiah 11:3 tells us, "His delight shall be in the fear of the Lord." That's why. *Therefore*, he shall not judge by what his eyes see or decide disputes by what his ears hear. Human appearances and opinions did not intimidate him or entice him. He was free to live in absolute abandon to the truth. "His delight [was] in the fear of the Lord," not the face of man. He didn't need the vain approval of others. He had found full and lasting satisfaction by standing in awe of God. That is the key to being a radically truthful person.

The glory of Jesus Christ is our final home. How did Jesus in the book of Revelation draw out the truth of Isaiah 11? He took his identity from verse 1 ("a *shoot* from the stump of Jesse") and from verse 10 ("the *root* of Jesse") and put it like this in Revelation 22:16: "I, Jesus . . . am the *root* and the *descendant* of David, the bright morning star." Not just the *descendant*—the shoot and branch of Isaiah 11:1—but also the *root* of David (Isa. 11:10). I am his source and his offspring. I am his father and his son. I am the beginning and the end.

This is how Jesus stumped the Pharisees with his own identity ("If then David calls him Lord, how is he his son?" Matt. 22:45), his preexistence ("Before Abraham was, I am," John 8:58), and his incarnation as the Son of David (Luke 1:32).

Home at Last

And what is the destiny of this God-man? Isaiah 11:10 declares, "In that day the root of Jesse, who shall stand as a signal for the peoples—of him shall the nations inquire, and his resting place shall be [*glory*]." When all his work of judgment and salvation is done, he will enter his rest, his final home, and one word will describe him and it: *glory.*

This glory is the sum of all the beauties of his person—all his wisdom and understanding and counsel and might and delight and righteousness and mercy. And this glory is the sum of all the beauties of his work—nations gathered, Israel restored, curse removed, new heaven, new earth, no harm, no destruction anymore. This is his resting place. Its name will be "glory" and he will be the center. And for all who have come to the signal, every sorrow will be past and every joy imaginable will be satisfied in him. We will be home. Amen.

Come, Lord Jesus.

3

THE LORD IS THERE

Ezekiel 40–48

D. A. CARSON

If we were to ask ourselves, "How on earth do we apply Eze-kiel 40–48 to the Christian church today?" we would be asking an important question. But it would not be the most important question. Better to ask, "How can we read these nine chapters in such a way that we internalize them, absorb them, so that they call up in imagination the vision that Ezekiel passes on, and respond the way that Ezekiel wanted his first hearers to respond?"

In other words, our task is more than a matter of coming from the outside and deciding which interpretation is correct, though there are some responsibilities along those lines. Rather, we must get inside the text so that the text, as it were, challenges us. The aim is not so much to master this apocalyptic text as to be mas-tered by it.

I shall take five steps. The first two merely gather some pre-liminary information, and the last three lay down the marrow of these chapters.

Step 1: The Outline of Ezekiel 40–48

Probably some of us have not read these chapters recently. Perhaps a few have never read them. In any case, this is not one of the best-known parts of the Bible, so let me presume on your patience and outline the chapters for you.

1. *Vision commission (40:1–4)*. The setting is fourteen years after the destruction of Jerusalem (586 BC), that is, about 572 BC. The leadership of the northern tribes was transported by the Assyrians about a century and a half earlier. In 597 some of the aristocracy of Judah, the southern two tribes, along with some nobles and priests were carted off to Babylon, transplanted to the banks of the Kebar River. Included in their number was young Ezekiel. About four years later, in 593, he began to receive visions from God. Those visions continued until 587/586, when Jerusalem was destroyed. The burden of Ezekiel's message during that time was roughly this: "Jerusalem has had it. It's under the judgment of God. It's going to be crushed. The Davidic dynasty will not be on the throne anymore, and the temple will be destroyed."

Can you imagine what that sounded like to the Israelites, who, like Ezekiel himself, were in captivity in Babylon? If he was right, then pretty soon they would have no home to go home to. This prevailing message of threatened judgment continues all the way until Ezekiel 33. At that point someone comes to Babylon with a report that the temple has fallen and the city has been destroyed. From then on, most of the messages in the book of Ezekiel are positive and offer promises and therefore hope to a captive people who would otherwise be in despair. Our section, Ezekiel 40–48, is one major part of this stirring up of hope.

2. *Restoration of the entire temple area (40:5–47)*. Before we can conceive of a new temple, there must be restoration of the entire temple area.

3. *Description of the new temple itself (40:48–41:20)*. In 40:48 to the end of chapter 41, the new temple itself is described, including its large-scale dimensions, shaped like the ancient tabernacle

and like Solomon's temple. The building is three times as long as it is wide: the Holy Place is twice as long as it is wide, and the Most Holy Place at one end, behind the veil, has a floor plan that is a perfect square. In fact, this room, the Most Holy Place, is a perfect cube, as high as it is long and wide.

4. *Rooms for the priests (chap. 42).* These rooms were used for preparing and eating the sacrifices, and for robing and disrobing, since the priests were not to use their priestly clothes outside in the common marketplace. The priests were to make a distinction between the holy and the profane.

5. *The glory returns and the altar is restored (chap. 43).* The chapter is divided into two parts. First, the glory returns. It is important to remember that in Ezekiel's earlier visions, the visions full of judgment and impending doom, the glory of God had abandoned Jerusalem (chaps. 10–11). Now the glory returns to the rebuilt temple. And then in 43:13–27, the altar is restored—that is, the place where sacrifice is offered up to God: the morning and the evening sacrifices, the sacrifices of Yom Kippur, the sacrifice of Passover, special sin offerings, and so forth.

6. *The priesthood is restored (chap. 44).* Chapter 44 focuses on the ceremonial restoration of the priesthood. Various stipulations are enumerated as to who is allowed to be priest: the priest must be a descendant of Zadok, of the line of Aaron. He also must be pure and free from outrageous sin.

7. *Israel is restored (chaps. 45–46).* That is to say, more and more steps are taken to renew the people of God. So 45:9–10 reads: "This is what the Sovereign LORD says: You have gone far enough, princes of Israel! Give up your violence and oppression and do what is just and right. Stop dispossessing my people, declares the Sovereign LORD. You are to use accurate scales, an accurate ephah and an accurate bath."[1] In other words, the government, the rule

---

1. Unless otherwise indicated in the text, Scripture references in this chapter are taken from The Holy Bible, New International Version®, NIV®. Copyright © 1973, 1978, 1984, 2011 by Biblica, Inc.™ Used by permission. All rights reserved worldwide.

of the prince, the monarch, is to maintain justice in the city—no crooked deals, no crooked scales, no oppression, and no violence. And then 45:17 says, "It will be the duty of the prince to provide the burnt offerings, grain offerings and drink offerings at the festivals, the New Moons and the Sabbaths." They were so to order their lives and the lives of the people that the appropriate sacrifices—the animals, wood, and needed accouterments—would all be provided for the temple. So important was the maintenance of temple ritual that the entire city was to work together in this respect under the administration of the king. And verse 21 adds, "In the first month on the fourteenth day you are to observe the Passover, a festival lasting seven days"—thus restoring these festivals that had been blotted out by the sack of the city.

8. *The river from the temple (47:1–12)*. This is a spectacular description, cast in evocative metaphorical terms.

9. *The boundaries of the division of the land (47:13–48:35a)*. In 47:13 to almost the end of 48, Ezekiel stipulates the boundaries of the divisions of the land, and they are highly schematized.

10. *Jerusalem gets a new name (48:35b)*. That name, finally, is disclosed in 48:35b: *Yahweh Shammah*—"the LORD is there."

So that's the outline of these chapters.

Step 2: Interpretations of Ezekiel 40–48

I must now outline some of the interpretations of these chapters. As you can well imagine, there are profound interpretive differences of opinion. Four of these predominate.

LITERAL SHORT-TERM PROPHECY

Some take Ezekiel 40–48 to be a literal short-term prophecy. They adopt a literal, prophetic, short-term interpretation. What you have in these chapters, they say, is a blueprint of the temple when Israel returns to the land after the exile. But if that is so, one has to admit the vision has not been carried out. More importantly, we have to remember that the entire vision is a unity. Chapters 40–48 constitute one block, and this unified vision includes numerous transparently symbol-laden elements.

For example, recall the river that begins as a little trickle from the south side of the temple, and then, without any mention of tributaries or the like, expands and grows and becomes ankle deep and then knee deep and then waist deep. It's heading downhill to the Arabah, toward the Jericho area, then into the Dead Sea. And when it gets to the Dead Sea, it turns the Dead Sea into fresh water. There cannot be many interpreters who take that description literally. Moreover, there is unreality to some of the borders and boundaries that would be easy to see on a chart or map. In other words, some degree of symbol-ladenness is embedded in the vision of Ezekiel 40–48—enough to make us query an interpretation that appeals primarily to a literal reading.

SYMBOLIC CHRISTIAN INTERPRETATION

On a second kind of reading, these chapters provide a symbol-laden description of the church from New Testament times all the way to the new heaven and the new earth. All of these chapters are fulfilled symbolically in the church now and in the consummation. There may be some truth to this (more on this later), but such direct reference to the church does seem a little bit forced.

DISPENSATIONAL INTERPRETATION

Somewhat akin to the first option, though not understanding these texts as being fulfilled when Israel returns to the land after the exile, dispensationalism tends to expect them to be fulfilled quite literally at the end of the age, in the expected millennium. The Scofield Bible, for instance, tells us, "Israel is in the land during the kingdom age." That's the summary of these chapters. In other words, again we expect literal fulfillment, but not in the short-term.

Some of us have difficulty with this view because of the expectation of a rebuilt temple with full temple rites and services many centuries after Jesus. How is that possible this side of the death and resurrection and priestly ministry of Christ, this side of the epistle to the Hebrews? Many dispensational writers would reply, "These institutions—temple, sacrifice, priesthood, and so on—look back on Christ and his cross in the same way in which these same institutions in the Old Testament looked forward to Christ and his cross. Thus they are not jeopardizing the exclusiveness of Christ and his cross." So those of us in the Reformed heritage must be careful not to charge these writers with something they disown. But I confess I remain unconvinced by this interpretation. The epistle to the Hebrews announces Jesus as a new High Priest in the order of Melchizedek, with the Levitical priesthood forever declared obsolete (Heb. 8:13). Moreover, we have to do with a heavenly tabernacle, the text says, not with a tabernacle built in Palestine. And the sacrifice of Christ described in Hebrews 9 in particular is clearly the ultimate sacrifice of Yom Kippur, the Day of Atonement.

Even if these sacrifices were to take place in an alleged millennium, they are not effective, according to the best dispensationalists. Yet it seems very odd to reintroduce them at all when they have so obviously been suspended because they have been superseded by that to which they pointed—a sacrifice that *is* effective. More importantly, under the terms of the new covenant, Jesus establishes until the end of the age one memorial rite that he thinks is important. We call it Holy Communion or the Lord's Supper or the Eucharist. That's the memorial rite, the ongoing rite, which the church is to use to look back on the cross and re-establish covenantal vows. Moreover, I would also argue that the dispensational interpretation has the same problems as the first interpretation. It does not handle well that part of the vision that seems to be hugely symbolic and apocalyptic.

Prophetic-Apocalyptic Interpretation

Before I outline a fourth interpretation, I should mention that if you hold some other view, most of what I will say in the following pages could be integrated into any of the earlier interpretations, but it best coheres with this option. We'll call this view the prophetic-apocalyptic interpretation. After all, the book of Ezekiel is not quite your usual prophetic literature; that is, the prophecy of Ezekiel has some of the characteristics of Old Testament prophetic literature, but it also has some of the characteristics of apocalyptic literature, so we can think of it as prophetic-apocalyptic. In the Old Testament, parts of Daniel are like that; similarly, there are four chapters in Isaiah that are sometimes called the Isaiah apocalypse (Isaiah 24–27). In the New Testament, of course, the book of Revelation, along with occasional chapters elsewhere, is often designated apocalyptic or prophetic-apocalyptic.

This fourth interpretation is somewhat akin to the second. The second understands the church as fulfilling all the symbolism of Ezekiel 40–48. This fourth interpretation takes a step back. It argues that Ezekiel is given a vision of the coming messianic age, a vision that lies in the future of Ezekiel's time but grows out of the categories present to Ezekiel's time. In short, the vision of Ezekiel 40–48 is largely cast in the tangible, old covenant terms that belong to the sixth century before Christ. Yet these are merely the forms in which new covenant blessings are being anticipated. As one writer puts it, "The vision of the temple was in fact a kind of incarnation of all that God stood for and all that he required and all that he could do for his people in the age that was about to dawn."[2] I will tease out more of this approach in the remaining steps.

Step 3: Ezekiel 1–39

Before studying Ezekiel 40–48, it is helpful to grasp something of the chapters that precede this material, namely, Ezekiel 1–39. We won't go into great detail, but I want to underscore a handful of elements.

2. John B. Taylor, *Ezekiel*, Tyndale Old Testament Commentaries (Downers Grove, IL: InterVarsity Press, 1969), 247.

Sennacherib was the marauding monarch of the Assyrians in the eighth century BC who finally destroyed Israel, the northern ten tribes. He then tried to destroy Jerusalem, the capitol of Judah, the southern two tribes, but God mercifully spared the city. Vast numbers of Assyrians were killed. Assyria never again marched south, trying to overpower Jerusalem. Indeed, by the time Ezekiel takes up his pen to write, the Assyrian empire is no more. It has been displaced by the Babylonians, the new regional superpower.

We have arrived at a period about 140 years later. The prophet Ezekiel is a contemporary of Jeremiah, who discharges his ministry back in Jerusalem. Ezekiel preaches to the exiles in Babylon. Though their respective audiences are different, their messages are similar. They keep denouncing the people of Jerusalem, warning that their sins will result in the utter destruction of the city. Yet the sin multiplies; defiance of God and his Word prevails. Corruption, idolatry, power politics, cruelty, systemic idolatry, drunkenness, hedonism, moral relativism—all these and many other sins grow bolder and more public, even as the city is squeezed harder and harder by the rising forces of the regional superpower, the kingdom of Babylon. Therefore Jerusalem will be punished. Ezekiel's version of this burden from the Lord warns the exiles, who hunger to escape from Babylon and return to Jerusalem, that the citizens of Jerusalem are so degenerate that Jerusalem cannot possibly stand.

This makes no sense to the Israelites who are in exile. How could God let Jerusalem go? It is the city of the great king. Moreover, everyone knows that in the past God has worked miraculously to spare the city: read again the account of Sennacherib (2 Kings 17). God miraculously spared the city in the past: wouldn't he do the same thing again, for his name's sake? And didn't he promise that there would always be a king from the Davidic line on the throne? How could the city fall and David's line be suspended? And besides, Jerusalem is the city of the temple—the place where God meets with his people, where God chose to manifest himself.

This is where sinners approach the living God by the sacrifices that God himself ordained. Do you really think God can forsake this city? If he were to do that, he would be abandoning his own covenant people—and that is unthinkable. Yet the constant message of Ezekiel, dominant in chapters 1–7, is "You don't understand. The people are worse than you think. And God has had enough. Judgment is decreed."

Then we arrive at Ezekiel 8–9. The depiction of the idolatry taking place in Jerusalem is appalling. What does corrupt worship look like? Start at 8:5. In Ezekiel 8 the prophet has been transported, whether in the body or out of the body, God knows (to use Paul's terminology), seven hundred miles from his home on the Kebar River back to Jerusalem. And there he is given a vision of the sheer perversity of the idolatry in the land.

Verse 5 says: "'Son of man, look toward the north.' So I looked, and in the entrance north of the gate of the altar I saw this idol of jealousy." We don't know what this "idol of jealousy" is. Whatever its identity, it is an idol that provokes God to jealousy. After all, the law declares, "For the LORD your God . . . is a jealous God" (Deut. 8:15). He does not put up with competitors. He insists on loyalty to the living God himself, to the living God alone. Anything less is idolatry.

So we read in Ezekiel 8:6, "And he said to me, 'Son of man, do you see what they are doing—the utterly detestable things the Israelites are doing here, things that will drive me far from my sanctuary?'" That is, God says, in effect, "Either holiness prevails and I stay, or sin prevails and I go. But you can't have it both ways."

> "But you will see things that are even more detestable."
> Then he brought me to the entrance to the court. I looked, and I saw a hole in the wall. He said to me, "Son of man, now dig into the wall." So I dug into the wall and saw a doorway there.
> And he said to me, "Go in and see the wicked and detestable things they are doing here." So I went in and looked, and

I saw portrayed all over the walls all kinds of crawling things and unclean animals and all the idols of Israel. In front of them stood seventy elders of Israel, and Jaazaniah son of Shaphan was standing among them. Each had a censer in his hand, and a fragrant cloud of incense was rising.

He said to me, "Son of man, have you seen what the elders of Israel are doing in the darkness, each at the shrine of his own idol? They say, 'The LORD does not see us; the LORD has forsaken the land.'" (8:6b–12)

These serpent deities and other idols are known to us from Babylonian, Canaanite, and Egyptian sources. What is on display is not only formidable syncretism but the worship of things that the Bible declares unclean.

Then God immediately adds, "You will see them doing things that are even more detestable" (8:13). And Ezekiel continues his description: "Then he brought me to the entrance of the north gate of the house of the LORD, and I saw women sitting there, mourning the god Tammuz. He said to me, 'Do you see this, son of man?'" (8:14–15).

Tammuz was a Sumerian god of vegetation who, according to Sumerian myth, died and became a god of the underworld. The cult connected with Tammuz incorporated a kind of mourning ritual in which the worshiper wept in the autumn when Tammuz passed away again and then ritually rejoiced in fertility in the spring when Tammuz came back to life. Such fertility cults were not uncommon in the Middle East of Ezekiel's day. Eventually, Tammuz wore Greek dress and came to be identified with Aphrodite. More than a century earlier, Isaiah had condemned the people of his day for planting Tammuz gardens (which is what the Hebrew literally calls them in Isaiah 17). Moreover, fertility cults were often excuses for sexual promiscuity that God deplores. A farmer might sleep with a priestess and his wife might sleep with a priest in order to encourage the copulation of the gods that would, in turn, bring productivity upon the land. The point is that here these people trust the fertility gods for their harvest and not the living God. "Do you see all this, son of man?"

But there are still more detestable things. Ezekiel 8:15 and following depict the crowning display of all that is detestable in worship. The setting is the very entrance to the temple itself, in the inner court, between the altar and the temple portico. The temple lies on an east-west axis. And this is enough to trigger, of all things, sun worship. With their backs to the temple, these people face east to worship the rising sun, in line with the Egyptian god called Ra. Not many years before this vision of Ezekiel 8–9, King Josiah removed the horses that the kings of Judah had dedicated to the sun (2 Kings 23). But now sun worship is back.

Corrupt worship replaces and relativizes God. The same is true, of course, today. Corrupt worship is not so much a question of the wrong method or the wrong style as the wrong god—a domesticated god perhaps, a syncretistic god, a compromised god. But none of these gods is the God who has disclosed himself. Our culture is not tempted by exactly the same idols and godlets that fed the fancies of the citizens of Jerusalem in the sixth century BC. I doubt if there are many people in the West who have been caught recently weeping for Tammuz. But some of the parallels will make us more uncomfortable than we might initially think. We do not set up Asherah poles and call them idols of jealousy. But if our heart devotion is drawn to anyone other than God himself, are we not provoking him to jealousy? We do not worship snakes, but do we not sometimes cherish and revere things that God declares unclean? Most of us, I suspect, are not engaged in fertility cults, but we come close to worshiping sex itself. Most of us have not worshiped the sun recently, but we are sold out to worshiping the creation rather than the Creator. And insofar as the sun represents for many people the ideal of endless vacations and pleasure and sun tan, maybe we worship the sun too, if just a wee bit.

But the next thing you must see in the book of Ezekiel is that the description of idolatry is followed by a description of judgment.

This promise of sure judgment on Jerusalem in the first part of chapter 11 is followed by a depiction of startlingly calloused indifference. In 11:14–15 we read, "The word of the LORD came to me: 'Son of man, the people of Jerusalem have said of your fellow exiles and all the other Israelites, "They are far away from the LORD; this land was given to us as our possession."'" In other words, while the people in Babylon are saying, "We so wish we could go home and see our families again and enjoy worship in the temple of our God," the people back in Jerusalem are saying, "Huh! *They* were deported. *They* must have been the bad guys. God had it in for them. They have no part with us now. *We're* the people in the pot. We're the good guys. We're the people whom God cherishes."

But in 11:16, God provides Ezekiel with a radically different analysis of the exiles: "Therefore say: 'This is what the Sovereign LORD says: Although I sent them far away among the nations and scattered them among the countries, yet for a little while I have been a *sanctuary* for them in the countries where they have gone.'"

That's *temple* language. God is making the Israelites in exile see that their access to the living God does not finally depend on stonework and masonry. God chose to disclose himself in the temple, whose dimensions, structures, sacrificial systems, and priesthood he had ordained. But at the end of the day, God's people must not put that mediating structure—which God graciously put in place—in the place of God. "It is enough," God essentially says, "that *I* be your sanctuary. So whether you are in Jerusalem or on the banks of the Kebar River, I will be a sanctuary for you; I will be your temple."

Within that framework, then, Ezekiel 36 announces the dawning of a new covenant whereby people's hearts are transformed. Ezekiel 37 and the valley of dry bones pictures the time when God will bring his people together like a resurrection. And then in 37:24–28, we find the promise of the dawning of a new covenant under King David.

This prophecy of Ezekiel opened with the vision of chapters 1–3; it closes with the climactic vision of chapters 40–48. In the first of these two visions, Ezekiel sees a mobile throne chariot. One of the reasons why it's *mobile* is that God is disclosing himself, in this vision, not in Jerusalem, but in Babylon. Most of the symbolism bound up with the design of the chariot is pretty straightforward. But then, as the vision begins to focus on the God who is sitting on the mobile throne chariot, the symbolism gets vaguer and vaguer until Ezekiel 1:28 says, "This was the appearance of the likeness of the glory of the LORD."

Now, try and draw that! I can draw the mobile throne chariot; I can't draw God.

In this spectacular inaugural vision of God, the mobile throne chariot is carefully introduced, but it plays no further role in Ezekiel's prophecy until chapters 8–11. There, as we've seen, Ezekiel witnesses in another vision the tragic and wretched idolatry that characterizes Jerusalem. After the description of idolatry in chapter 8, the glory of the Lord that is hovering over the temple—signifying the presence of God, at the God-ordained place of meeting through the God-ordained sacrifices and the God-ordained priesthood—this glory leaves the temple and sits on the mobile throne chariot.

Then the mobile throne chariot leaves the city. It goes out through the gates, crosses the Kidron Valley, climbs the mountain, and parks on the Mount of Olives and watches what will unfold. The purpose of this vision is to assert, in this symbolic fashion, that if Jerusalem falls, it's not because Emperor Nebuchadnezzar is so strong that poor God does not have a chance. If Jerusalem falls, it's because God has decreed its fall by his judicial abandoning of the city. The only reason that Nebuchadnezzar could take the city is that God abandoned it to its God-ordained judgment.

But now in the final vision of the prophecy of Ezekiel (chaps. 40–48), the prophet sees a renewed Israel, a renewed city, a spectacular temple. That's the way the book of Ezekiel ends.

Step 4: The Burden of Ezekiel 40–48

So now we come to the burden of chapters 40–48. I will summarize it in two main points. And then I will briefly indicate in the fifth step some of the ways in which the New Testament picks up the strands in these chapters.

Both Already and Not Yet

First, typical of many prophecies after the exile, Ezekiel simultaneously sees both the promise of soon restoration to the land and the promise of ultimate restoration in the transformed world still to come. Prompted by the Spirit of God, Ezekiel peers into the future. The cascading mountain ranges in front of him enable him to see both near and distant vistas, but he cannot tell the extent to which these vistas are separated; he cannot see how deep and wide are the valleys that separate these mountain ranges.

The prophet can see the return at the end of the exile, and he can also see the glory yet to come at the end of the age. How many ridges there are is not always clear; indeed, because the prophet is standing far enough back, he sees these vistas as one mass, such that he can leap from one to another and back again.

So these chapters provide prophecies of return from exile, but they also provide vistas of the time when the spectacular water of life transforms the Dead Sea and turns it into a sea of life. Along the banks of this flow of transforming water there is fruit all through the year, and the leaves of the trees on both banks serve for the healing of the nations—which is a vision that John the seer, in the last book of the Bible, picks up. Moreover, the description of the river in Ezekiel 47:1–12 is laden with Eden images. For example, observe the watering of the land (compare Gen. 2:10) by the rivers that bring forth fruitfulness in Eden. The blessing extends, then, to the whole land and beyond.

GODLY WORSHIP RESTORED

Second, the perfection of God's plan to restore his people is symbolized in the perfect symmetry of the temple precincts, the temple courtyards, the temple wall, and the temple building, and the precise ordering of all the people. The centrality of godly worship in the coming new age is still cast in Old Testament categories as portrayed in the scrupulous perfection of God's ordained rites, the sinlessness of God's ordained priests, and the meticulous care to conform to God's prescribed sacrifices—all of these perfections standing over against the appalling perversion of worship earlier in the book. Just as the portrayal of perverse worship— the perverseness of idolatry—was cast in old covenant terms, so now the overthrow of such perversion is still cast in old covenant terms. We begin to see what right worship looks like, with God at the center, with God-ordained sacrifices, with the God-ordained priestly system, in the God-ordained temple—all cast in old covenant categories with mind-bending images thrown in to show that the reality outstrips the symbolism, all the way to the water of life that awakens the Dead Sea to life. In short:

- In pure worship, God is not relativized. He is not an avocation; he is not a hobby. It is possible to join six thousand voices in a large conference and feel as if you are on the threshold of heaven as you stand and sing "In Christ Alone," all the while thinking, rather pathetically, "I wonder if the person next to me admires my bass voice?" We all recognize that when we worship God with our money, a sneaky thought insinuates itself to tell us how wonderfully generous we are; when we worship God by ordering our lives in godly priorities, we may cast a guilty glance around to see if anyone is noticing; and when we join together in exuberant, joyful, corporate worship, a part of us discounts what we are experiencing because we have to return to humdrum existence the next day. We want to be God-centered, truly, but most of us go through life fearing that people will think too little of us rather than fearing they will think too much of us—exactly the reverse of Paul (2 Cor. 12:5–6). But one day, God will not be relativized, not in anything we say or think or do, no matter the work we're given to do. That will be pure worship—not so much because the worship itself is intrinsically pure, but because the God whom we worship will then be so clear before our eyes, that it is simply unthinkable to worship anything else.

- That which aspires to be pure worship in a broken world is bound to be countercultural. Ezekiel understands that. He doesn't assume the return to the land will automatically guarantee perfection. Rather, in several passages he says, in effect, "If you abandon your idols, and if the priests maintain their purity, and if the king ensures the maintenance of the covenant, you will be spared further exile; you will be blessed by the presence of God." Do you see what this means? It means that God's people expect to live differently from the surrounding peoples. They realize that they cannot possibly fit into the culture of the region, because the culture—I don't care which culture—is not God-centered. The best Christian worship is intrinsically countercultural. It is intrinsically reforming, because such worship has massive moral implications. That's why in Ezekiel 40–48, we read things like this: "This is what the Sovereign LORD says: You have gone far enough, princes of Israel! Give up your violence and oppression and do what is just and right. Stop dispossessing my people, declares the Sovereign LORD" (45:9). Or again: "This land will be his possession in Israel. And my princes will no longer oppress my people but will allow the people of Israel to possess the land according to their tribes" (45:8). And much more of the same.

THE ULTIMATE GOAL

But above all, the goal of these nine chapters is found in the very last line: The name of the city from that time on will be *Yahweh*

Shammah. Write it on a card and affix it somewhere you can see it often: *Yahweh Shammah*—"The LORD is there."

At funerals we sometimes lay quite a bit of emphasis on the fact that Christians never say their last good-bye. Death means we will be reunited with loved ones who have died in the Lord before us. My mother died of Alzheimer's and complications proceeding from that dreadful disease. During the last couple of years, she never said anything. Six months before she died, we could sing old hymns, such as "Face to Face with Christ, My Savior." And we'd get a little squeeze of the hand. During her last months, there was no observable response at all. Some day, I tell myself, I shall ask her, "Did you hear us? When we prayed for you, did you hear us? Can you remember our singing, our recitation of biblical passages?"

Indeed, it's right that I should think like that and contemplate renewed relationships with Mum and Dad and with other loved ones who have gone into glory ahead of me. But such expectation is wrong if it is at the expense of longing for God. For when you read Revelation 21–22, the glory of the place is not bound up with visiting your mother. It's not about having a theological tête-à-tête with the apostle Paul so as to ask him just what he meant by the end of Romans 11. It's all about God: "The Lord is there." That is why the vision of Ezekiel 40–48 ends the way it does; that is why across the vistas of church history the ultimate good is often described in two Latin words: *visio Dei*—"the vision of God." The Lord is there.

If this prospect elicits only the weakest sympathetic vibration within us, it's because our present understanding of God is just too small.

That brings me to the last step.

Step 5: Ezekiel 40–48 and the New Testament

Where do we go after chapters 40–48? Seventy years later the temple is rebuilt—a much smaller building. More striking is the fact that there is no report of glory descending upon the temple. Glory settled on the tabernacle of the time of Moses, and glory settled on the temple of the time of Solomon, but there is no mention of glory settling on this rebuilt, small-scale temple that made old men weep because it was so pathetic compared with the Solomonic version.

The returned exiles tried to rebuild the city, but the Emperor Xerxes wouldn't let them (Ezra 4). Twenty years later, God raised up Nehemiah and eventually the city was rebuilt and repopulated. So they had the city of Jerusalem; they had the temple. But they still did not have a Davidic king on the throne: the regional superpower would not permit it. Decades rolled by, then centuries. The people of God who had been captured by the Assyrians and the Babylonians found themselves under the Persians, then under the Greeks, and finally, from 63 BC on, under the Romans. And still there was no king in David's line on the throne.

The True Temple

Then, you turn the pages to the New Testament. The first line reads, "The genealogy of Jesus the Messiah the son of *David*, the son of Abraham" (Matt. 1:1). This is the Jesus who declares, "Destroy this *temple*, and I will raise it again in three days" (John 2:19). If the temple is the true meeting place between God and his sinful people, this claim makes Jesus the ultimate meeting place between God and his people. Similarly, the evangelist John testifies, "The Word became flesh and *tabernacled* among us, and we have seen his glory" (John 1:14, my trans.).

Jesus is the ultimate temple, the ultimate tabernacle, the ultimate meeting place between God and his people. That's where the ultimate glory lies: in Christ Jesus, this Jesus who is glorified by being lifted up on a cross and dying a shameful death, the Just for the unjust, on his way to returning to the glory he had with his Father before the world began.

THE HOLY CITY

The last vision of the last book of the Bible depicts the seer John testifying, "I saw the Holy City, the new Jerusalem, coming down out of heaven from God" (Rev. 21:2). This city shone with the glory of God. In this vision, the New Jerusalem boasts striking symmetries that remind one of the huge symmetries in the visions of Ezekiel. But in this city there is no temple, "because the Lord God Almighty and the Lamb are its temple" (Rev. 21:22). Isn't that what God had told the exiles on the banks of the Kebar River? He said, "I will be a sanctuary for you." Then, in words reminiscent of the prophecy of Ezekiel, John writes:

> Then the angel showed me the river of the water of life, as clear as crystal, flowing from the throne of God and of the Lamb down the middle of the great street of the city. On each side of the river stood the tree of life, bearing twelve crops of fruit, yielding its fruit every month. And the leaves of the tree are for the healing of the nations. No longer will there be any curse. The throne of God and of the Lamb will be in the city, and his servants will serve him. They will see his face, and his name will be on their foreheads. (Rev. 22:1–4)

WRITTEN ON THEIR FOREHEADS

In the book of Ezekiel, only those who had the name of God written on their foreheads were spared the judgment. The similar words from Revelation are a way of saying this is the fulfillment of that earlier vision. These people are in the new heaven and the new earth, the New Jerusalem, and they have God's name on their foreheads. "There will be no more night. They will not need the light of a lamp or the light of the sun, for the Lord God will give them light. And they will reign for ever and ever" (Rev. 22:5).

But do not neglect verse 4: "They will see his face." In the book of Revelation, even the highest order of angels cannot look on God. The angelic beings of Revelation 4 can't look on God. They hide their faces with their wings. The only ones who can look on

God are God's image bearers, now so transformed that they see his face and live. For indeed *Yahweh Shammah*, "The LORD is there."

> Only faintly now I see Him,
> With a darkened veil between,
> But a better day is coming,
> When His glory shall be seen.[3]

Yahweh Shammah!

3. Carrie E. Breck, "Face to Face with Christ, My Savior," 1898.

4

THE FATHER'S HOME, AND THE WAY THERE

John 14:1–14

AUGUSTUS NICODEMUS LOPES

Jesus speaks the words of John 14:1–14 to his disciples in the upper room on the night he is betrayed. Earlier, Jesus entered Jerusalem as the long-awaited King of the Jews, riding a donkey, for the Feast of Passover (12:12–19). Some Greeks came to see him during the feast. Jesus knows now that the time has come for him to suffer and die for his people—both Jews and Gentiles (12:20–26). At the same time, the Jews, under the Pharisees, scribes, and the high priest, increase their opposition to Jesus, refusing to believe in him as the Messiah, the Son of God—despite the many signs he has done (12:27–50).

He then turns his attention to his disciples, those who have believed and followed him. He brings them to the upper room, where he begins to prepare them for his passion and departure to the Father. Jesus washes their feet, pointing to their spiritual cleansing by his blood (13:1–20). He separates the traitor from among them, and Judas goes away after Satan enters him (13:21–30).

Then Jesus begins to instruct his disciples as to what is about to happen and the things that are to come, and he starts by telling them he is about to depart from them and go where they cannot follow him, although they will follow latter. He gives them a new commandment: to love one another (13:34–35). Peter, then, becomes very disturbed by Jesus's words about his going away from them. And Peter grows even more anxious when Jesus says that Peter will deny him no fewer than three times that very night (13:36–38).

These events set the stage for Jesus's well-known farewell discourse. His practical purpose on that night, at that moment, is to calm the disciples' anxiety. In doing that, he teaches them about the Father's house and the way there.

Five-Part Division

John 14:1–14 can be divided into five parts. First, Jesus tells his disciples to not be troubled (14:1). Second, he gives them three reasons for not being troubled: there are many rooms in his Father's house (14:2); he is going there to prepare a place for them (14:2b–3a); and he will come back and get them to be with him forever (14:3). Third, he teaches them the way to the Father's house (14:4–6). Fourth, he tells them they can enjoy the Father, here and now, before going to the Father's house, by faith in him, Jesus (14:7–11). And, finally, in addition to knowing the Father, here and now, they will be able to continue Jesus's ministry by faith in him (14:12–14).

I'll try to unpack each of these parts.

Part 1: Let Not Your Hearts Be Troubled

Jesus says in verse 1, "Let not your hearts be troubled. Believe in God; believe also in me." Even though Jesus himself is troubled, as we read in 12:27, he is still concerned to help his friends. This shows the heart of our Savior; even in the midst of his trials, he is attentive, caring for those who are his.

As already mentioned, the disciples are troubled with two

things Jesus has just said. The first is that he will soon leave them and go to a place where they cannot find him. Jesus is referring to his imminent death. They do not understand that yet. Still, they feel sad that Jesus is going to leave them and that they will not be able to find him. They are not only sad but also confused and perplexed. How does Jesus's departure fit within the expectation they have that he is the one who will bring about the long-awaited kingdom of God?

The second cause of their unrest is Jesus's affirmation that Peter will deny him no fewer than three times that night. It's not difficult to imagine the turmoil in their hearts, the shame, the fear. That is why Jesus says at first: "Let not your hearts be troubled." Then, he tells them, "Believe in God; believe also in me" (14:1).

The meaning of what Jesus is saying here appears to be this: to believe in God and believe in Jesus Christ would free the disciples from the unrest they feel when thinking about Jesus's imminent parting and Peter's denial. They should believe Jesus just as they should believe in God, because Jesus and the Father are one. As God, Jesus would never leave them alone, nor would he abandon Peter after his fall. Jesus's claim of being God is the very foundation of their hope and comfort.

PART 2: THREE REASONS WHY YOU SHOULD NOT BE TROUBLED

Jesus continues: "In my Father's house are many rooms. If it were not so, would I have told you that I go to prepare a place for you? And if I go and prepare a place for you, I will come again and will take you to myself, that where I am you may be also" (John 14:2–3). Jesus gives three reasons here for the disciples to have peace in the midst of perplexity.

First, *there are many rooms in the Father's house*. This saying raises two questions: What is the Father's house? And what is the meaning of the "many rooms"?

I believe Jesus is saying that, after his death and resurrection, he will go to heaven, the place where the Father is, the place of his dwelling. Jesus calls it "my Father's house" not only to comfort the disciples with a cozy metaphor but also perhaps in contrast to the temple of Jerusalem, the earthly house of God, from which the disciples will soon be expelled.

The "many rooms" in the Father's house simply means that there is enough room there for them and for all who will come later, for those Greeks who want to see Jesus, along with all the other Gentiles and Jews who will later believe—even us.

The second reason for them not to let their hearts be troubled is that *Jesus is going to prepare a place for them* (14:2). And, of course, another important question is What is this "preparation"? We should not imagine that the Lord Jesus Christ is in some way right now building mansions or houses for us in heaven. He is not even improving or repairing what has been ready since the foundation of the world. He says in the Gospel of Matthew to those who will be saved, "Come, you who are blessed by my Father, inherit the kingdom prepared for you from the foundation of the world" (Matt. 25:34). The writer of Hebrews says, in reference to God's rest, "His works were finished from the foundation of the world" (Heb. 4:3). So what then is this preparation?

I believe Jesus's death and resurrection are themselves the preparation. He is going to prepare a place for them, and for us, by going there through his death and resurrection. The rooms are ready, but we are not able to get in. Jesus prepares a place for his people by dying on the cross for their sins. He opens the way to the Father's house and if this were not so, he would have told them. Therefore, what would seem a cause for a great unrest in their hearts is actually the opposite. It is reason for joy, hope, and comfort. His departure is necessary for our entry into the Father's house.

The third reason Jesus gives them not to be troubled is this: *after he has prepared a room for them, he will come back to take them and receive them, and they will be together forever.* He says, "And if I go and prepare a place for you, I will come again and will take you to myself, that where I am you may be also" (John 14:3).

Here Jesus tells his disciples why he will come to take them back. But several questions in this passage deserve closer attention, especially these two: When will Jesus come back to take them? And what does it mean that they will stay with him forever?

Let's look at the first question: When will Jesus come back to them, according to verse 3? Throughout the history of the church, people have given different answers to this question. Some have said that Jesus means his resurrection. Others, that he comes back to his disciples in the Spirit on the day of Pentecost, and he is with us to this very day. Others say that Jesus comes to us when we die, as he came to meet Stephen when the Jews stoned him to death (Acts 7:56). Others contend that Jesus is talking about his second coming, and still others say that the statement is intentionally vague to accommodate all these possibilities.

I think the best interpretation is that Jesus is referring to his second coming. Of course, this does not exclude the other comings, because the idea of Jesus coming to his disciples occurs several times in John, with all these meanings. The idea of the second coming fits better in the context of Jesus saying, in essence, "I will come back from my Father's house; I'll take you with me, and we will be together forever." In other words, Jesus is basically saying, "Let not your hearts be troubled; I'm going to die, yes, but I will live again, I will go to heaven, and then I will come back publicly, openly, before the eyes of the whole world, to take you to be with me forever." I think this is the best explanation.

This raises the next question: Where exactly will Jesus's people be together forever after his return? As we read the text, it appears that Jesus is going to return from the Father's house to receive them. And it is there, in the Father's house, according to the flow of the text, that they will stay together forever. Notice that Jesus says, "I will come again and will take you to myself" (John 14:3).

In a very good sermon on this passage John Piper points out that Jesus is not concerned about a place; his main concern is his own person. He is coming to take them to himself. So the text is about being with Jesus.

It appears from verse 2 that the Father's house is heaven, the place of God's dwelling. But as we know, heaven is not our final destination! We are not going to stay in heaven forever. It is an intermediate state. So in verse 3, Jesus seems to expand the meaning of the Father's house to include the new kingdom, the new world he is going to bring about upon his return, where he will stay forever with his people. Heaven will continue on earth. The Father's house, in other words, seems to be God's kingdom, both heaven after death and the new heaven and new earth, where we shall be with Jesus forever. And what binds these two stages together is that Jesus will be there.

We may apply here what John Piper and Don Carson have said in previous chapters, about prophecy being like seeing two or three mountains in one. When Jesus speaks of the Father's house, he has in mind not only heaven where he will go after his death and resurrection—and where we go after we die—but also the new heaven and the new earth, which are, in a way, a continuation of heaven.

In this way Jesus comforts his disciples' hearts, pointing to the kingdom that we enter after we die and where we shall live forever.

PART 3: THIS IS THE WAY TO THE FATHER'S HOUSE

The passage continues:

> "And you know the way to where I am going." Thomas said to him, "Lord, we do not know where you are going. How can we know the way?" Jesus said to him, "I am the way, and the truth, and the life. No one comes to the Father except through me. If you had known me, you would have known my Father also. From now on you do know him and have seen him." (John 14:4–7)

At first, Jesus seems to assume that his disciples know what he is talking about, that they know where he is going and the way there. It is not difficult to understand why Jesus says what he does. He has been teaching them for three years about God's kingdom, his own unity with the Father, and the need for one to believe in him to have eternal life.

Thomas's reaction, however, seems to show that the disciples are not quite sure what Jesus is saying. Thomas, speaking for the others, declares openly that they don't know where Jesus is going and, therefore, they have no idea how to get there (14:5). Now, we should not think that Jesus has mistaken his disciples' level of understanding. Remember that they are consistently depicted in this Gospel as slow of understanding and as frequently misunderstanding Jesus's words. So Jesus probably wants to provoke a reaction that will allow him to present himself as the way to the Father's house: "I am the way, and the truth, and the life. No one comes to the Father except through me" (14:6).

Not only is he going to the Father's house to prepare a place, but he himself is the way there, the only way through which the disciples can come to the Father's house. Moreover, because he is the way, he is also the truth and the life—the truth because he is God's perfect revelation of how a lost world can come to God, and the life because only in him can the world find life eternal. And that is the reason he says no one comes to the Father except through him. He is the Lamb of God, who takes away the sin of the world. Nobody else has done this. Jesus will give his flesh to eat and his blood to drink for the life of his people. So this is why he is the way, the truth, and the life.

If the disciples had really understood who Jesus is, they would have already known he is the way to the Father and to the Father's house, as he says in verse 7: "If you had known me, you would have known my Father also." There is a rebuke here, even if a mild one. They should know by now that Jesus is not only the Messiah, the Son of God, but also God's perfect revelation—he is God himself. To see Jesus, then, is the same as to see God; therefore, to believe, to know, to see Jesus is to really know, see, and come to the Father and his house. Jesus Christ is the way there, the way to the Father.

PART 4: KNOWING THE FATHER HERE AND NOW

An exchange between Philip and Jesus follows:

> Philip said to him, "Lord, show us the Father, and it is enough for us." Jesus said to him, "Have I been with you so long, and you still do not know me, Philip? Whoever has seen me has seen the Father. How can you say, 'Show us the Father'? Do you not believe that I am in the Father and the Father is in me? The words that I say to you I do not speak on my own authority, but the Father who dwells in me does his works. Believe me that I am in the Father and the Father is in me, or else believe on account of the works themselves." (John 14:8–11)

Philip seems to be asking for a kind of vision of God, like Moses asking God: "Please show me your glory" (Ex. 33:18). Apparently Philip wants a theophany or a manifestation of God's glory, such as the burning bush.

For Philip, if God would just appear to the disciples, the matter would be settled. No more explanations would be necessary. All would be crystal clear. God's appearance would be sufficient for them to face the coming trials, the shame, and the fears. "Let me see God; I want to see God," he basically says. His request is likely provoked by what Jesus has said in John 14:7: "From now on you do know him and have seen him." When Jesus says "from now on," he is probably referring to the period after his death and resurrection.

When Jesus says that Philip is going to see him now, Philip answers in effect: "Well, this is what I'm talking about! Go ahead and show us—show us the Father! And that'll be enough!" Jesus's reply, however, is that the encounter with God that Philip is asking for has already been happening for three years. "Have I been with you so long, and you still do not know me, Philip? Whoever has seen me has seen the Father. How can you say, 'Show us the Father'?" (14:9).

How is it possible, after all that time, that Philip and the others have not yet understood that Jesus is God and that to see him is to see God? God has been there all along, beside them! They have touched God; they have spoken to God; they have laughed together with God; they've eaten and drunk with God; they've walked miles and miles with God, side by side!

Apparently, Philip and the others do not lack faith in God and in Jesus. They lack a full understanding of Jesus's divinity and that he is the full and perfect image of the invisible God, the radiance of his glory, and the exact imprint of his nature.

Jesus then asks Philip and the others to believe that he, the Son, is in God and God is in him on account of two things. First are the words Jesus speaks, words that have come from the Father: "I am in the Father and the Father is in me[.] The words that I say to you I do not speak on my own authority, but the Father who dwells in me does his works" (14:10). So, what Jesus wants for them to do is to believe in him on account of the words because these words come from the Father. But not only words.

Jesus also wants them to believe because of the works the Father is doing through him: "Believe me that I am in the Father and the Father is in me, or else believe on account of the works themselves" (14:11). By works, no doubt, Jesus means, primarily, signs and miracles. That is evidence enough that God is in him— evidence such as walking on the water, multiplying bread and fish, turning water into wine, and resurrecting the dead.

But, of course, "the works" may include more than just the signs. The phrase may also refer to Jesus's love, obedience to the Father, compassion for sinners, and ministry toward the poor. Jesus's life and works can only be explained if God is in him. If the disciples believe Jesus is in God and God is in him, based on the works they have observed in Jesus for three years, they will see God here and now, even before going to the Father's house. And what a comfort for troubled hearts!

PART 5: YOU WILL DO EVEN GREATER WORKS

So Jesus concludes:

> Truly, truly, I say to you, whoever believes in me will also do the works that I do; and greater works than these will he do, because I am going to the Father. Whatever you ask in my name, this I will do, that the Father may be glorified in the Son. If you ask me anything in my name, I will do it. (John 14:12–14)

Now, let's pause for a moment and remember the main practical goal of John 14:1–14. Jesus is trying to quiet the turmoil of his disciples' hearts. He tells them he is going to prepare a place for them in his Father's house, where there are enough rooms for them and others. Jesus says he will come back to take them and be with them forever. He also says they already know the Father and see the Father by faith in him, in Jesus—here and now. And now, Jesus tells them that, by faith in him, they will be able to continue his ministry after he has gone to the Father. And what a great comfort for troubled hearts! Jesus presents them with a confident future in which they will continue the Master's work.

There are several points to be noticed in this remarkable passage, but I will keep myself to what seem to be the two main points.

The works they will do. First, what are the works that Jesus is talking about when he says, "Truly, truly, I say to you, whoever believes in me will also do the works that I do" (14:12)? No doubt, miraculous signs are in view. We should not try to exclude this meaning because of our commitment to a theological view that does not allow for signs of any kind today. Often this commitment is an overreaction to the wrong way in which this passage has been read and used by false teachers and false prophets today.

At the same time, we should consider that signs are merely a piece of the whole, and maybe even a small one. The term "works" is broader than "signs" in the Gospel of John. Works can also include, as I mentioned before, what Jesus has done: preaching, teaching, ministering to the poor, and (yes) doing miracles. And all this will be done not only by the Twelve but also by all those who believe in him.

How are these works greater? Second, in what sense will the work of those who believe in him be greater? Of course, the most popular interpretation of this passage is that Christians who have enough faith are able to do greater miracles than Jesus did. This is a very widespread interpretation of the passage, at least in Brazil, where the Pentecostal and New Pentecostal churches greatly outnumber the Reformed and historical churches. Even though it seems easy to tell and show people that no miracles done today come close to walking on water, multiplying bread and fish, and raising a man dead for four days, this misinterpretation continues unabated in those circles.

The key to understanding what Jesus says can be found in the reason he gives to his disciples and in his promise to them concerning these works. They will be able to do the same works he did and even greater works because he is going to the Father: "Truly, truly, I say to you, whoever believes in me will also do the works that I do; and greater works than these will he do, *because* I am going to the Father" (John 14:12). "Going to the Father" means Jesus's exaltation after his death and resurrection, and the inauguration of the new era marked by the outpouring of the Holy Spirit at Pentecost.

Thus, in terms of redemptive-historical sequence and fulfillment, the times after Jesus's death, resurrection, and exaltation are greater. As a consequence, the works done by his disciples after those events will also be greater, not necessarily in number, extension, and power, but primarily because of their salvation-historical character. As Don Carson explains in his commentary on John, the signs would have more clear meaning and reach their full purpose, and everything would now be done in the light of Jesus's death and resurrection. This is why they would be greater.[1]

Now, look at the promise Jesus makes to his disciples. Our Lord tells them he will answer their prayers in his name—anything they ask to the glory of the Father: "Whatever you ask in my name, this I will do, that the Father may be glorified in the Son. If you ask me anything in my name, I will do it" (14:13–14).

We should notice that this promise is not a blank check for you to fill up with anything you want. This promise is given in the context of another, a promise about doing the works of Jesus. Jesus appears to mean this: in the process of doing these works, he will be ready to answer our prayer to be like him, to have power to do his works, to minister to people, to announce the gospel, to have compassion on the poor. We must not isolate this promise from its context. It is a promise related to the one about greater works.

Jesus continues to do his work today. When we put these two points together, we get this: Jesus will continue to do his work after he returns to the Father to be glorified. And he will use the disciples to continue to do his works. What Jesus does before his death and resurrection is the beginning of his works, according to the introduction to the book of Acts (Acts 1:1), with the clear implication that the acts of the apostles are what Jesus continues to do through them after his resurrection. He is going to send the Holy Spirit upon them with power for that purpose.

Thus, the works of his disciples will be greater because they will do them over a longer span of time, a more glorious period, the new era that dawns with the Lord's resurrection. They will also reach the world, while Jesus's ministry was local. They

---

1. D. A. Carson, *The Gospel according to John*, The Pillar New Testament Commentary (Grand Rapids, MI: Eerdmans, 1991), 496.

bring a greater number of people to the kingdom, as Peter saw on the day of Pentecost. And, of course, they perform signs and wonders. God can do the same today if he so wills. But the promise is related to the continuation of Jesus's ministry. In other words: we can experience in the present world, by faith in Jesus, the powers of the world to come. To do the works of Jesus in the present is a great comfort and a guarantee that Jesus will come back for his people to stay with them forever in the Father's house.

What Can We Learn?

What are the implications of this passage for the difficult times the church is experiencing across the globe? I'm thinking specifically about the persecution that is coming to our brothers and sisters in some parts of the world. We should not to be ashamed to comfort our hearts and the hearts of those under persecution with the hope that Jesus offers here. He points to the future: "Let not your hearts to be troubled!" And he points to the Father's house.

Some people call religion the opiate of the people. Karl Marx had Christianity and our eschatological hope in mind when he said that. Some contend that pointing to the future as the Christian's ultimate hope tends to make us to forget the needs of the present world. They argue that if you have your mind in the clouds, you forget your feet are on the earth. And so we have been criticized, and sometimes rightly so, because we forget that we have to do something here and now.

Still Our Blessed Hope

While this disregard for the world may have been the case at some times in church history, we should not be ashamed to say that the hope of the Christian is the blessed hope of the new heaven and the new earth. Our hope is not here; it is not from here that we get our comfort. There is nothing on earth power-

ful enough to quiet the turmoil in our hearts. The hope that is
given us in the Bible is the hope of the *eschaton*—the coming
kingdom of God.

What are the implications of this text for the role of the church
in political and social reconstruction, for example? The text shows
that the way Jesus's disciples impact the world is by doing his
works, and greater ones, here and now. And that, of course, as
we mentioned, includes acts of compassion and love for those
who suffer, and most certainly—as Jesus did—calling on sinners,
big and small, to repent of their sins and believe in Jesus for eternal life. Most of us understand that unrepentant sinners cannot
be reconstructed. Or course, we believe in common grace, but
we know that common grace does not convert sinners. Only the
gospel does.

Gifts of the Spirit Today

What is the bearing of this text on the debate about the gifts of the
Spirit today? I believe this passage teaches us to admit that God
can work miracles today in answer to the prayers of his people. But
it also teaches that signs should not be our main concern. Philip
wanted to have an immediate vision of God: Jesus responded with
the incarnation!

What is the impact of this text as to whether there is salvation
in other religions? Is there salvation outside of Christ? Will all
people be saved in the end? Our passage gives us an unequivocal
answer to all these questions: there is no salvation outside of faith
in Jesus Christ. The Father's house is only for those who believe
Jesus Christ is the Son of God, our only Savior.

What about the Eschatology Debate?

What about the ongoing eschatological debate? The text teaches
that the essence of our eschatological hope is to be with Jesus
forever, and it does not matter if it is in a millennium or not. The
point is this: our hope is his person, his presence. This should

moderate the tone of our discussion about eschatology and season with love the way we disagree with one another.

What about the Here and Now?

And, finally, what is the calling of this text for you and me, right now? How do you know that you have a key to those rooms in the Father's house? There is only one answer in the light of this text: those who believe in Jesus will do his works.

Do I see these works being done through me? Is Jesus working today through me in answer to my prayers? Do I have love and compassion for others? Do I seek God's glory as Jesus did? This is the only way we can assure ourselves that we know the way, the truth, and the life. And in this way alone do we know that among those places, among those many rooms in "my Father's house"— in Jesus's Father's house—there is a place for me.

5

THE DAY OF THE LORD

1 Thessalonians 4:13–5:11

MARK DEVER

Allow me to introduce you to Secular Sam. Secular Sam is very successful. He has a good job, a nice girlfriend, a beautiful apartment, a new car, and excellent health. He's humorous, intelligent, and personable. Secular Sam is also a Christian, and actually he is quite an active one. He has an evangelical background (though he has chosen to leave behind some of the embarrassing bits of this background), is theologically conservative, and believes in the authority of Scripture.

Indeed, he's even come to see Scripture as the most satisfying explanation for all kinds of phenomena, from the origin of the world to the meaning of life. Sam, being a student of Scripture, can realistically examine humanity's sinfulness. He can even confute his secular friends with historical evidence for the resurrection. He knows that all of life is under the scrutiny of God's Word: not just his religion, but also business, philosophy, ethics, economics, and law.

What is it, then, that makes Secular Sam so secular? Sam is secular because he expects to wake up in his bed tomorrow morning. He's never even heard of what his grandparents called "the blessed hope." Sam's hopes and concerns, even about his own spiritual life, are all contained in this *seculum* (the Latin word from which we get "secular"), that is, this age and this life. Sam assumes that tomorrow will be just like today, and that has some serious implications for the way he thinks about today.

In 1851, a nineteenth-century Englishman named George Holyoake was the first to propose a system called secularism. Through his journal, *The Reasoner*, Holyoake taught that morality should be based solely upon a regard for the well-being of mankind in this present life, without consideration of any belief in God or a future state. Of course, such secularism is really of great antiquity; it's much older than Holyoake and *The Reasoner*. But from the shapers of the ancient pagan world to those of the modern pagan world—Darwin, Marx, and Freud—secularism has flourished.

Even granted the basic human belief in some kind of age or life after this one, we can easily understand how, in a society at large or in an individual, a kind of creeping unbelief can gain the upper hand. One may begin by believing in this age as well as the next, but he will soon begin concentrating on this age rather than the next, emphasizing this age rather than the next, being concerned with this age rather than the next, thinking less of the next, de-emphasizing the next, questioning the next, ignoring the next, forgetting the next, and finally, denying the next. As our churches do more and more to help us cope with this life and less and less to help us prepare for the next, this secularism has grown in both the society and the church.

In 1 Thessalonians 4:13–5:11, the apostle Paul raises two problems with such secularism. First, he examines the hopelessness of secularism, and second, he examines the immorality of secularism.

The Hopelessness of Secularism

First Thessalonians, perhaps the earliest of Paul's letters, indicates that the effects of secularism have existed even from the very beginning among young Christian churches, which at the time of

Paul's writing are just ten or fifteen years old at most. In our passage, the problem Paul identifies first is a hopelessness among the Thessalonian believers. The problem is that their ignorance about death—here referred to by the metaphor of falling "asleep"—is causing them to "grieve as others do who have no hope" (4:13).

Isn't that true of many people's experiences? There are so many people who live with no hope and think like the secularist Bertrand Russell, who, in his essay "A Free Man's Worship," wrote, "The life of man is a long march through the night, surrounded by invisible foes, tortured by weariness and pain, towards a goal that few can hope to reach, and where none may tarry long."[1] That is materialism, the belief that matter is all that exists; or as I've also heard it defined, "a stupid philosophy in which people invest everything in what will one day become nothing."

WE DO NOT GRIEVE AS THOSE WITHOUT HOPE

Paul's answer, however, is that Christians do have a hope: the dead are still in Jesus! "Since we believe that Jesus died and rose again, even so, through Jesus, God will bring with him those who have fallen asleep" (1 Thess. 4:14). It's because of the Christian's connection with Christ that we have hope in the face of death, for our hope is bound up in him.

The first funeral at which I ever officiated was in Florida more than thirty years ago, and though I did not know the deceased very well, I knew he was not a professing Christian. His death had been a complete surprise, and I was called on short notice. I found myself standing around the casket of a man I barely knew with a small crowd of people, most of whom I did not know at all. I began to wonder, "Why me? Why am I, a young man in his early twenties, preaching to this crowd of strangers?" But I realized that it was because I have this hope: I know someone who has gone

---

1. Richard A. Rempel, Andrew Brink, and Margaret Moran, eds., *The Collected Papers of Bertrand Russell*, vol. 12, *Contemplation and Action: 1902–1914* (London: George Allen & Unwin, 1985), 71.

into the grave and come back out. That's why I was there at that funeral. It was not because I knew the departed man but because I knew One who died and rose again. It's because Christ died and rose again that we can have the hope that if we're in Christ, even if we die, we will rise again.

Paul writes of God "bringing" those who have died in Christ—that is, those who have died as Christians—with Jesus. The word for "bring" that Paul uses here is a word used of someone who is alive, not someone who is dead. But here Paul speaks hope to the Thessalonians based on their union with Christ. Death, he says, doesn't break this union with Christ.

Friend, if you have had a Christian brother or sister, husband or wife, or father or mother or child depart, there is hope in this truth that the union we have with Christ is more basic than this life itself. Even as Christ died and rose, we too—as those united with Christ—will die and rise again. Those who die in Christ will, as it were, come back "with him" when he returns.

GOING TO MEET A KING

The Thessalonians are worried that they have no hope because some of them have died before Christ has returned, but Paul assures them that the very opposite is true: "For this we declare to you by a word from the Lord, that we who are alive, who are left until the coming of the Lord, will not precede those who have fallen asleep" (1 Thess. 4:15).

To describe this coming of the Lord, Paul uses the word customarily used for official visits of Roman emperors to provinces when they would come to display their sovereignty over an area. When the emperor would visit a city, a delegation would be sent out from the city to greet the emperor first. Paul, by using that imagery, is showing the Thessalonians how the dead in Christ will be like a delegation going to meet the coming Lord, and so will actually have precedence over the living. So much for being hopeless. The dead in Christ will be the first to receive the returning King!

In using this official, royal, military imagery, Paul writes of this event that no one has yet witnessed: "For the Lord himself will descend from heaven with a cry of command, with the voice of an archangel, and with the sound of the trumpet of God. And the dead in Christ will rise first" (4:16).

There is a similar image in Exodus 19, where Moses meets with the Lord at Mount Sinai. God descends from heaven onto the mountain, surrounded by thick clouds with the trumpet sounding, and he is met with a procession of people out from the camp led by Moses. Here in 1 Thessalonians, Paul says the Lord himself will come down from heaven "with a cry of command, with the voice of an archangel, and with the sound of the trumpet of God," but this time it won't be Moses alone who goes up to meet the Lord, with the others just standing away down the mountain as a part of the procession. Instead, it will be all Christians. We are part of that privileged procession that will meet with the Lord. Those who have died in Christ are far from being left out of the festivities; they lead the way.

The dead in Christ, says Paul, will rise first. As for those who are alive in Christ, he adds in 4:17, "we who are alive, who are left, will be caught up together with them in the clouds to meet the Lord in the air." We too, if we are Christians, will rise and ascend at Christ's return even as he once did.

You Were Made to Know God

Here is the wonderful summary of our hope: "and so we will always be with the Lord" (1 Thess. 4:17). If you are reading this and are not a Christian, know that there is a great hope that you can have. Friend, you were actually made for a purpose: you were made to know God. All the frustrations you experience in life are part of God's kindness showing you that this life is not all there is. This world is too small to fit the hopes of a creature made in his image, and that means you.

God made you and me, and even though we have sinned

against him and he is rightly offended by our wrongdoings, he loved us enough to send the Lord Jesus Christ, his only begotten Son, to live a perfect life and die on the cross as our substitute.

Don't miss that fact, because if you want to understand Christianity, you need to understand the strange idea that a person can act on behalf of another. Then you will understand that we're all sinful because Adam sinned, and we were all "in" Adam—that is, represented by him—and we have ratified that choice by our sinful actions.

But in God's amazing grace, when he could've destroyed Adam and Eve for their rebellion and ended humanity there, he instead decided to send his only Son, Jesus Christ. Christ laid down his life voluntarily for all of us who would turn from our sins and trust in him, and after God raised him from the dead, Christ ascended to heaven and presented his sacrifice to the Father. The book of Hebrews tells us how the Father accepted this sacrifice, and in accepting that sacrifice he has accepted all of us who will trust in Christ alone. Friend, this hope to "always be with the Lord" can be yours today. What better hope is there to have? What more would you spend your life on?

The Immorality of Secularism

Paul knows the Thessalonians' confusion about the coming age presents another danger besides hopelessness. Secularism, as we have seen, recognizes only this life and nothing beyond the grave. But if we keep reading, Paul in 1 Thessalonians 5 also speaks of the immorality of secularism and points out that the real problem is not with those who have died in Christ. The real problem is with those who live in darkness.

> Now concerning the times and the seasons, brothers, you have no need to have anything written to you. For you yourselves are fully aware that the day of the Lord will come like a thief in the

night. While people are saying, "There is peace and security," then sudden destruction will come upon them as labor pains come upon a pregnant woman, and they will not escape. But you are not in darkness, brothers, for that day to surprise you like a thief. For you are all children of light, children of the day. We are not of the night or of the darkness. So then let us not sleep, as others do, but let us keep awake and be sober. For those who sleep, sleep at night, and those who get drunk, are drunk at night. But since we belong to the day, let us be sober, having put on the breastplate of faith and love, and for a helmet the hope of salvation. (1 Thess. 5:1–8)

The Thessalonians have been instructed concerning "the day of the Lord," which is a prominent theme in the Old Testament. It is the day which, in a peculiar sense, belongs to God. Of course the Lord owns all of time and all days, but there is one that in a peculiar sense is the property of God. On that day, he will make himself perfectly clear to the world and complete his work. That is the great day in which nature seems to expire: the sun is darkened, the moon turns blood red, the stars vanish, and there are earthquakes, storms, disasters, fire, and smoke. It's the great day in which God's people are delivered from their enemies and the hypocrites are finally sifted out from among the Lord's people. God's rule is finally, utterly revealed. The wicked enter into eternal punishment and God's grace to his people reaches its climax. It is the end of this *seculum*, this age, and the full beginning of the new.

In the New Testament, we see that this day of the Lord is the return of Christ. Paul notes that the Thessalonians have been well instructed about all of this, so he has no need to write about the "when" of it all. But those outside of Christ, says Paul, are not only hopeless but also tragically clueless about this coming day of the Lord. Their ignorance of that coming age means they are in for a big surprise. What's worse, their ignorance and their surprise at that day will ensure their destruction.

THEY WILL NOT ESCAPE

I enjoy reading history. I remember reading A. G. Gardiner's essays on the First World War, written not long after the war had ended. He described the terrible rapidity of events surrounding the beginning of the Great War, as it was called. If you've ever studied it, you know it began almost accidentally. He writes:

> We were indifferent [to the goings-on in Europe before the outbreak of the war], because in our happy security, we thought they had no bearing upon our lives. We find that we were wrong. . . . As I write in a tiny hamlet of a Midland county, I look across to a little cottage and see a woman bending at work in the garden. Last July she had three sons. To-day, two of them lie in unknown graves in Flanders. The third is wounded and in hospital. I dare to say she did not so much as hear of the Sarajevo tragedy [that began World War I]. Yet that tragedy lighted a train of events that has wrecked her life as it has wrecked the lives of millions all over the face of Europe. . . .
>
> . . . The swift and tremendous drama that unrolls . . . is as though with a careless remark about the weather we stumble upon the Day of Judgment.[2]

Even more suddenly will the real day of judgment come, says Paul. The day of the Lord will come like a thief in the night. "While people are saying, 'There is peace and security,' then sudden destruction will come upon them, as labor pains come upon a pregnant woman, and they will not escape" (1 Thess. 5:3). They may speak of security, but they won't have it. Calamity will come on them and overtake them, and all of a sudden everything that has seemed so peaceful and secure will dissolve under the awful weight of the Lord's return. The crack of doom will sound, and utter destruction will replace what they have taken to be the sure and certain world of material comfort. As Paul says with chilling clarity here in verse 3, "They will not escape."

---

2. Alfred George Gardiner, *The War Lords* (London: Dent, 1915), 115, 120.

ASLEEP OR ALERT?

Their ignorance leads even now to lives marked by spiritual slumber and drunkenness: "For those who sleep, sleep at night, and those who get drunk, are drunk at night" (1 Thess. 5:7). Paul describes them in 5:6 as asleep. For people very likely busily involved in their families, their jobs, and the many things of the world around them, these people the apostle has in mind would think of themselves as awake and aware. But to the day of the Lord that is certainly to come, they are asleep.

"But none of this should surprise you," Paul essentially says to the Thessalonian Christians. "You are awake and alert. You are not in the dark." Look again at 5:4–8:

> But you are not in darkness, brothers, for that day to surprise you like a thief. For you are all children of light, children of the day. We are not of the night or of the darkness. So then let us not sleep, as others do, but let us keep awake and be sober. For those who sleep, sleep at night, and those who get drunk, are drunk at night. But since we belong to the day, let us be sober, having put on the breastplate of faith and love, and for a helmet the hope of salvation.

So here we see the connection between alertness and self-control. If you need to be more self-controlled, inform yourself more of reality. Study the Word, see the truth, and learn the times we're living in. Being awake leads to that kind of self-control. Children of the light and the day are awake, alert, and aware. But alert to and aware of what? We are aware that the day of the Lord is coming, and that is the motivation, as Paul says here, for being self-controlled. We are to watch and be sober because we know what's coming, and part of staying alert means being self-controlled.

Spiritual slumber keeps you from realizing that the day of the Lord is coming. When you do realize the Lord is coming, as these believers do, it means not only that you shouldn't be surprised, but also that you should be living in the light of that knowledge even now. Those who are spiritually awake will know to be self-controlled and to be dressed with faith, love, and hope, because they will know that they must shortly give an account of their lives to their Creator.

On the other hand, those who are spiritually asleep, who are ignorant of the coming day of the Lord, will live in spiritual sleep and a drunken stupor, knowing no control, because they think they won't have to give an account. Since what feels good now is all that matters to them, how do you think they will live?

GOD JUDGES BECAUSE HE IS GOOD

In his book *Utopia*, Thomas More wrote of a perfect place bearing that name, which is visited by a traveler named Raphael Hythlodaeus. Hythlodaeus reports that three things have to be taken by all Utopians on faith: the immortality of the soul, reward and punishment after death, and the existence of providence. He explains:

> Anyone who thinks differently in their view has forfeited his right to be classed as a human being by degrading his immortal soul to the level of an animal's body. Still less do they regard him as a Utopian citizen. They say a person like this doesn't really care for the Utopian way of life, he's only too afraid to say so. Where it stands to reason that you're not afraid of anything but prosecution, and have no hopes for anything after you're dead, you'll always be trying to evade or break the laws of your country in order to gain your own private ends.[3]

So Hythlodaeus answers our question of how those who are spiritually asleep will conduct themselves. Unless they believe in a final judgment, natural law will have no effect on them. Why practice self-control if there is no punishment for not doing so?

Scripture affirms this connection. If God were to extend his patience and forbearance forever, how would that be any differ-

---

3. James J. Greene and John P. Dolan, eds., *The Essential Thomas More* (New York: Mentor-Omega, 1967), 87–88.

ent from moral indifference? God judges not because he must but because he will, and because he is completely good.

Alexis de Tocqueville, writing about his visit to the United States in the early 1800s, said, "Hitherto, no one in the United States has dared to advance the maxim that everything is permissible for the interests of society,—an impious adage, which seems to have been invented in an age of freedom to shelter all future tyrants."[4] We have seen this in our own lifetime. We've seen the total rejection of the idea that we must give an account to our Creator for the lives we live.

A 1987 article in *Policy Review* by Joshua Haberman, a Jewish rabbi living in Alabama, was titled "The Bible Belt Is America's Safety Belt." In this interesting article, Haberman complained about the overwhelmingly negative portrayal of American fundamentalist Christians by the culture and media of the time. Where he lived, he was surrounded by fundamentalist Christians, he said, and considered them to be great neighbors because they believed they would have to give an account to God of their lives. If they stole or committed murder, God would see and judge them, and because of this belief, they lived controlled and moral lives. By contrast, said Haberman, it wasn't Christian fundamentalism that held sway in Russia or Germany before the terrible tyrannies of the twentieth century.

Having fled from Vienna in 1938 because of the rise of Nazism there, Haberman could assert from personal experience that it was no accident that Hitler's Third Reich and the Soviet state both identified the Bible and its teachers as primary enemies. So, he concluded, the Bible is far from a threat to our freedoms. It is America's safety belt.

I'm not sure what Haberman would say today, thirty years later. But as Christians, we are to live like the rabbi commends, showing by our actions that we know we will have to give an

---

4. Alexis de Tocqueville, *Democracy in America*, trans. Henry Reeve (New York: Barnes and Noble, 2003), 278.

account to God. That should be reflected in all we do, and the truth is that it will be by the way we choose to live. Examine your life and ask yourself by what expectation you live. Why do you do the things you do? What hope is moving you?

Together with Him

Let us conclude by looking at 1 Thessalonians 5:9–11: "For God has not destined us for wrath, but to obtain salvation through our Lord Jesus Christ, who died for us so that whether we are awake or asleep we might live with him. Therefore encourage one another and build one another up, just as you are doing."

Paul concludes by encouraging these young Christians with the fact that the future is good for them. They look forward not to wrath and the terrors of judgment but to salvation: "For God has not destined us for wrath, but to obtain salvation through our Lord Jesus Christ" (5:9). The final victory will be ours! But even now we are blessed, because Jesus died so that we may live together with him, both then and now, whether alive or dead at his return: "[He] died for us so that whether we are awake or asleep we might live with him" (5:10).

As Christians, we are called to the high privilege of living with the Lord now and forever. Life is not like a car with no driver, careening out of control and going quickly to nowhere; nor is it like a ravenous beast, led by its cravings and appetites but with no meaning other than immediate gratification. Life has a purpose and a meaning given by God.

Are You Ready?

Finally, notice how Paul says to encourage one another with these words at the end of both sections in 1 Thessalonians 4:13–5:11. At the end of the first passage, 4:13–18, he tells us to encourage each other to hope, and in the second, 5:1–11, he tells us to encourage each other to morality. He leaves the duty of encouragement with those who preach. Preachers don't do everything; they just get things started. If the church is healthy, its people feed off the Word of God (see Deut. 8:3) and share it with one another, and encouragement reverberates through the local church.

Early one morning in 1833, a frightened little boy ran to his mother saying, "Oh mother, the world is coming to an end! The stars are falling!" Startled from her sleep, the mother rushed to the window and saw what was probably one of the most remarkable meteor showers that ever occurred. One competent observer declared that he had never seen snowflakes thicker in a storm than there were in the sky some moments that day. The meteors made no sound and none were reported to have hit earth, but everywhere people were falling on their faces, thinking that the end of the world had come. But what did that mother say when she saw what she thought was the end?

"Thank God! I am ready!"

And friend, if you're ready for that, you're ready for anything. Are you ready? Are you living like it? Encourage one another, comfort one another, and exhort one another with these words.

6

THE RESURRECTION AND THE LIFE

1 Corinthians 15:35–58

VODDIE BAUCHAM JR.

First Corinthians 15:35–58 may be a weighty passage, but Paul's pastoral heart stands out in these words nonetheless. Most people see this as an apologetic section—and they're right—but there is also pastoral ministry happening here. There is a sense in which Paul is dealing with the doctrine of the resurrection from a practical, pastoral perspective.

Paul has provided a convincing apologetic for the doctrine of the resurrection, and he offers three lines of argumentation in order to prove his point. First, there is the argument from authority—what the Scriptures say—in 15:4. Second, there is the argument from evidence—the account of eyewitnesses, including himself—in 15:5–11. Finally, he offers an argument from logic: if there is no resurrection, seven things will follow as inexorably as night follows day. And after he has explained this, he goes back to the fact that he's already defended: Christ has been raised.

More Than Apologetics: The Resurrection Matters

Having won the day and proven his point, however, Paul is not content merely to stand triumphantly over the bodies of his defeated foes. This, for him, is about more than winning an argument. He moves beyond apologetics and returns to application. He goes from proving his point to pressing his point, from orthodoxy to orthopraxy. He goes from the fact of the resurrection to the reason why it matters. As the quintessential pastor and apologist, Paul takes the opportunity to shepherd the sheep toward their ultimate hope. And he does so via his oft-used practice of dealing with a question as though it were asked while he writes.

Paul does this in a number of places, including several large sections in the book of Romans. And here in 1 Corinthians he begins with "But someone will ask" (15:35). He has proven that the resurrection is true, and now he's proving that the resurrection is essential. And he doesn't do it in an ethereal way; he does it in a way that deals with a question that either has been asked before or he knows is going to be asked based on his understanding of the human condition and the way people relate to this kind of information.

But what does it mean to ask, "How are the dead raised? With what kind of body do they come?" (15:35)? We know what happens to things when they die. We know what happens to people when they die. We understand death. But we don't know what the resurrection looks like because we've never seen a resurrection. All we have is the record and testimony of the witnesses of the resurrection of Jesus Christ all those years ago. That's what prompted Calvin to write:

> There is nothing more at variance with human reason than this article of faith. For who but God alone could persuade us that bodies which are now liable to corruption will, after having rotted away, or after they have been consumed by fire or torn to pieces by wild beasts, will not merely be restored entire but in a greatly better condition. Do not all our apprehensions of things straightaway reject this as a thing fabulous, nay, most absurd?[1]

1. John Calvin, *Commentary on the Epistles of Paul the Apostle to the Corinthians*, vol. 2, trans. John Pringle (Grand Rapids, MI: Eerdmans, 1948), 46.

RESCUED FROM THE DEAD

I resonate with that. The first time I saw a dead body, I was seventeen years old and an unbeliever. I had never heard the gospel and would not hear it for another year or so after that. I was born to a single, teenage Buddhist mother and raised in drug-infested, gang-infested South Central Los Angeles, California. And when I was old enough to find a little trouble, or for a little trouble to find me, my mother shipped me out, and we kids moved from South Central L.A. all the way across the country—three days on a Greyhound bus—to Beaufort, South Carolina. There, we lived with her older brother, who was a retired drill instructor from the US Marine Corps. And I got out of trouble, quick, fast, and in a hurry!

Several years later, having moved to the great state of Texas, I got a phone call that my cousin Jamal was dead. All of a sudden I was reminded of the things that my mother had rescued me from by sending me away. I was reminded, as I contemplated my cousin, who was six months younger than I, and who had become a drug dealer, and who—depending on which stories are accurate—somehow found himself in a bad situation. At sixteen years old, he was shot in the back of the head and killed. I traveled back to Los Angeles and stood there over his body, and I had no hope. As I stood there, all I could think was "Is this the end? What do I have to look forward to other than this? What more is there than this?"

So I resonate with the notion that resurrection is not an easy idea for us to grasp. Yet Paul rebukes Corinthian unbelief. Yes, it's something difficult to grasp; however, this is something that God has said in his Word. It's one thing for an unbeliever not to have categories to deal with death. It's another thing for individuals who are associated with the church of the living God and who have heard about the death, burial, and resurrection of Jesus Christ to say, "I'm not sure that could happen." And so Paul calls them foolish people. He doesn't say, "Hey, I understand how difficult this is for you to grasp. I get that." He says, "You foolish person!" (1 Cor. 15:36).

This is not a mere insult. The language here is designed to press home a point, which is basically this: "You have the evidence of the Word of God. You have the evidence of apostolic preaching. But you also have the evidence of general revelation."

Yet someone will say, "I just can't comprehend how something could die and be buried and then come back again." "You foolish person!" Paul answers.

ALTERNATIVE ANSWERS?

Consider this: What did you eat today? It probably died and was buried in one form and came back in another form. God has shown you this not only in his Word but even through the things you see in nature, and yet you've determined not to believe. That means you have to accept an alternative answer, and what is that? Your alternative answer could be some form of Platonic dualism, Docetism, Cerinthian Gnosticism—some idea that matter is bad. And because matter is bad, this whole resurrection thing with Jesus wasn't really a resurrection at all. Either he wasn't really human, because God would not inhabit sinful human flesh, and he only appeared to be human, or he really was human, but his deity merely came upon him at his baptism and then left him there at the cross. But the idea that he is fully human is completely unaccept-able to this kind of dualistic thinking. And so if you're not going to believe the resurrection, you're probably going to believe some other explanation like this, and Paul refutes that.

If you're not going to believe the resurrection, what are you going to believe in? Reincarnation? That somehow this is just your earth suit, and you'll leave this earth suit and go to another earth suit, and it may be an animal, it may be a bird, or it may be a pig? And then you have to treat animals well, because they may very well be a dearly departed loved one? That won't do.

What about some kind of nihilism, the whole Lion King "circle of life" type thing—that it really doesn't matter at all? We die, and we go back to the dust, and we are consumed into this endless circle. There's a group called the Urban Death Project, and recently they floated the idea of using dead human beings as fertilizer. We use other dead things, why not use people?

The Resurrection Transforms Our Anthropology

You see, the first thing that resurrection life does for us is to address our anthropology, our understanding of the very nature of man. This doctrine affirms the dignity of humanity. The fact that Christ took on flesh, then died, was buried, and was raised again; that he did not merely discard his flesh and go back to his heavenly home; that he took this flesh with him in its resurrected form—all this says something about the inherent dignity of humanity in its entirety. Human beings as whole beings have inherent dignity.

All of this says something about the way we think of ourselves and others. It says something about the sanctity of human life at every point. God could have had his Son come in another way, but he did not. God could have skipped over those insignificant aspects of human existence, but he did not.

And so Christ comes into the womb of a woman and experiences the entirety of human development, thereby sanctifying it and saying to us that from the moment of conception, this is human life worth honoring. The resurrection teaches us this because Christ takes up that flesh again. Paul looks back to creation (Genesis 1) to make this point. Beginning in 1 Corinthians 15:39 he takes days four, five, and six of creation and orders them in reverse:

> For not all flesh is the same, but there is one kind for humans, another for animals, another for birds, and another for fish. There are heavenly bodies and earthly bodies, but the glory of the heavenly is of one kind, and the glory of the earthly is of another. There is one glory of the sun, and another glory of the moon, and another glory of the stars; for star differs from star in glory. (15:39–41)

So the glory of the human body is not the same as the glory of other things, not the same as the glory of other bodies. That's why even a nihilist will not pass by a dead human being and act like nothing is wrong. I don't care what you say you believe; if you see a fallen human being, you don't simply step over and walk by. Something in us understands this inherent dignity of humanity. This is why you can pass by a car accident, and if you were laughing and jovial and playing up till then, the moment you realize that someone has died, even though you did not know him or her, you're not the same. There is a unique glory associated with us, and the resurrection of Jesus Christ affirms this. It transforms our anthropology.

The Resurrection Transforms Soteriology

Not only does it transform our anthropology; it also transforms our soteriology. There is a bridge statement beginning in verse 42:

> So is it with the resurrection of the dead. What is sown is perishable; what is raised is imperishable. It is sown in dishonor; it is raised in glory. It is sown in weakness; it is raised in power. It is sown a natural body; it is raised a spiritual body. If there is a natural body, there is also a spiritual body. (1 Cor. 15:42–44)

So there's a sense in which the glory of the human body differs from the glory of other flesh, but there's also a sense in which the glory of the resurrected body differs from the glory of our bodies as they are now.

First Adam, Last Adam

To explain this, Paul introduces the contrast between the first Adam and the last Adam:

> Thus it is written, "The first man Adam became a living being"; the last Adam became a life-giving spirit. But it is not the spiritual that is first but the natural, and then the spiritual. The first

man was from the earth, a man of dust; the second man is from
heaven. As was the man of dust, so also are those who are of
the dust, and as is the man of heaven, so also are those who
are of heaven. Just as we have borne the image of the man of
dust, we shall also bear the image of the man of heaven. (1 Cor.
15:45–49)

Jesus has been resurrected and we're going to be resurrected.
Why? Because we are united with him! This is the idea of federal
headship. Paul has introduced the concept earlier in chapter 15,
but let me delve into it a little bit more. Paul asserts that the resurrection is real for us because our union with Christ is real for us.
We have actual union with Jesus Christ. And in fact, death for us
is the result of our union under the federal headship of Adam, so
that in Adam all of us died.

Our resurrection, then, is connected to the change of our
federal head. Why are we all guilty in Adam? For the same reason that we are all forgiven in Christ. Earlier, in verses 21–22,
Paul writes, "For as by a man came death, by a man has come
also the resurrection of the dead. For as in Adam all die, so also
in Christ shall all be made alive." This is why the virgin birth
matters. Jesus is not under the federal headship of Adam. This
is why those who say the virgin birth is unimportant are wrong.
And those who say Christ is merely our example are wrong. If
Christ is just our example and there was no virgin birth, then he
stands condemned because Adam is his federal head, which is
true for all those who are born by natural generation. However,
because of the virgin birth, Christ is not under that federal headship. This is why we must affirm his impeccability and can know
that Jesus did not sin.

PERFECT OBEDIENCE

A recent worldview survey found that some 45 percent of professing Christian teenagers believe that Jesus sinned during his
earthly ministry. I know two things: one, they don't understand

the gospel, and two, they're not being catechized. The most basic catechisms deal with this question. What kind of life did Christ live on earth? A life of perfect obedience to the law of God. Little kids are asked questions like this.

But we've come to believe that theology doesn't matter. Paul doesn't believe that. He believes the doctrine of the resurrection matters on a very practical level, because if you don't get the resurrection right, then you don't understand that you are under Christ's federal headship. And you don't understand the significance of his active and passive obedience, that in his active obedience he has kept the entirety of the law and is actually righteous. Thereby he is able to impute actual righteousness to you.

And in his passive obedience, Christ accepts in himself the debt that you owed to God but could not pay. Therefore, we can impute to him our sinfulness, and because of this double imputation, we stand before God under the federal headship of Jesus Christ not only forgiven but also righteous. And we can actually anticipate the resurrection of our bodies.

That doctrine matters. If Christ is not actually righteous, then he's no better than Buddha. He's no better than Gandhi. He's no better than Confucius. He's just an example, and you can take him or leave him. But if he was born of a virgin, lived a sinless life, died a vicarious substitutionary death, rose in a victorious, confirming resurrection, ascended to the right hand of God, is making intercession for us, and is one day going to return to judge the living and the dead, and is going to gather his people to himself to take them where he is, then this doctrine matters.

The Resurrection Transforms Our Missiology

Next we see how the resurrection life changes our missiology. Paul begins by using a familiar passage that parallels one already dealt with earlier. Let's start in verse 54:

When the perishable puts on the imperishable, and the mortal puts on immortality, then shall come to pass the saying that is written:

"Death is swallowed up in victory."
"O death, where is your victory?
   O death, where is your sting?" (1 Cor. 15:54–55)

YOUR DAY WILL COME

The last time I checked, the death rate was one per person. I didn't check today, but I'm sure it didn't change. It is appointed to man to die once, then face the judgment (Heb. 9:27). So everyone everywhere is asking or will ask the same question: How can I avoid being defeated by that last enemy? You can't beat him. You can't buy him off. You can't appease him. You can't outrun him. You can't exercise enough or eat well enough. There is nothing you can do to avoid being overtaken by this enemy.

But the resurrection says you can overcome this enemy: "O death, where is your sting?" You see, when you stand over a believer, it's not the same as standing over an unbeliever, because when you stand over a believer, you know that because of his union with Christ, his federal head, he will rise just as Christ rose from the dead. There is a resurrection coming. So this sting is gone; death's victory is gone.

BUT CHRIST DEFEATED DEATH

But there's more! "The sting of death is sin, and the power of sin is the law" (1 Cor. 15:56). Sin and the law have been dealt with by the active obedience of Christ. That's why this sting has been taken away.

But thanks be to God, who gives us the victory through our Lord Jesus Christ.

Therefore, my beloved brothers, be steadfast, immovable, always abounding in the work of the Lord, knowing that in the Lord your labor is not in vain. (15:57–58)

The question is What is this labor? Is this labor referring to anything we do? That's the way we usually read it. But I believe there is something more specific referenced here. Go back to verses 14–19. There, in his argument from logic, Paul presents something very similar:

> And if Christ has not been raised, then our preaching is in vain and your faith is in vain. We are even found to be misrepresenting God, because we testified about God that he raised Christ, whom he did not raise if it is true that the dead are not raised. For if the dead are not raised, not even Christ has been raised. And if Christ has not been raised, your faith is futile and you are still in your sins. Then those also who have fallen asleep in Christ have perished. If in Christ we have hope in this life only, we are of all people most to be pitied.

THE MINISTRY OF RECONCILIATION

So when Paul talks about our labor not being in vain, he is referring to our gospel ministry, our proclamation of the gospel, but also to our holiness and our life of faith. Later he says:

> I protest, brothers, by my pride in you, which I have in Christ Jesus our Lord, I die every day! What do I gain if, humanly speaking, I fought with beasts at Ephesus? If the dead are not raised, "Let us eat and drink, for tomorrow we die." Do not be deceived: "Bad company ruins good morals." Wake up from your drunken stupor, as is right, and do not go on sinning. For some have no knowledge of God. I say this to your shame. (1 Cor. 15:31–34)

Again, what are we talking about? The proclamation of the gospel and our life of faith and righteousness—this is the labor that is not in vain. The labor that's not in vain is gospel labor. This is a labor of righteousness because of the gospel and its impact on us. And we proclaim the gospel so that Christ might have the fullness of the reward for which he died. That's the labor that's not in vain. Is it because we're guaranteed success? No. Is it because we're guaranteed to transform our culture? No. Yet, we can labor in the gospel, persevere in righteousness, pursue holiness to the glory of God, and fail to achieve any of the outward things that we so desperately strive for, and still our labor has not been in vain.

FOUR REASONS OUR LABOR IS NOT IN VAIN

Why? There are four reasons. First, because our labor means that the true, effectual gospel goes forth, and that's never in vain. The proclamation of the truth of the gospel will always accomplish what God intended it to accomplish. So we pound away and pound away. Brothers, do not give up on proclaiming the gospel. That happens from time to time and from place to place where preaching the gospel just doesn't seem to get it done. And so we put our faith and our hope and our trust in various programs and means of manipulation, building a better mousetrap, trying to find out what we need to do to bring people in, because therein lies our success. No, our success is in our faithfulness in proclaiming the gospel. Do we want people to be saved? Absolutely! We want people to be saved by the millions, but not so we can say we are good at what we do, but so that we can say, "I rejoice in Christ having the fullness of the reward for which he died."

Second, when it is gospel labor, it conforms us to the image of Christ in true righteousness. There are back-to-back chapters in Romans that address this reality. In Romans 5, Paul discusses the idea of federal headship and the idea of the first Adam and the last Adam. But then he comes to chapter 6, where he asks another very important question. Let's look first at Romans 5:18–21:

> Therefore, as one trespass led to condemnation for all men, so one act of righteousness leads to justification and life for all men. For as by the one man's disobedience the many were made sinners, so by the one man's obedience the many will be made righteous. Now the law came in to increase the trespass, but where sin increased, grace abounded all the more, so that, as sin reigned in

104 Voddie Baucham Jr.

death, grace also might reign through righteousness leading to eternal life through Jesus Christ our Lord.

Then Paul says in chapter 6:

> What shall we say then? Are we to continue in sin that grace may abound? By no means! How can we who died to sin still live in it? Do you not know that all of us who have been baptized into Christ Jesus were baptized into his death? We were buried therefore with him by baptism into death, in order that, just as Christ was raised from the dead by the glory of the Father, we too might walk in newness of life. (6:1–4)

So the resurrection is not just so we can get up on that great "gettin'-up" morning. The resurrection is also a picture of us walking in the newness of life we have right now. Why? Because that resurrection life is mine right now. Martha learns this when she essentially says, "Oh Jesus, if you had just been here, my brother wouldn't have died! I know you could've done something, but now it's too late!" (John 11:21). Jesus doesn't have any "one day" statements for her. He doesn't even say that he's going to call on his Father. What does he say? "I am the resurrection and the life" (John 11:25). Whoever believes in Christ, death is not enough to hold them. And if Christ is the resurrection and the life, then resurrection life is not something I just look forward to—though it is that. There is also a sense in which that resurrection life is a current reality, this "already, not yet" reality in which we walk. Why? For holiness. For righteousness. For hope.

Third, our labor prepares us for his coming. I remember the first time I preached at a funeral and it dawned on me that the pastor is not just an administrator, hand-holder, preacher, or counselor. I stood there, and for the first time I had shepherded someone to the grave. I realized that's what we do. We're so used to people just getting up and leaving a church because they don't like the color of the carpet or the music or the preaching, but sometimes people don't go voluntarily. Sometimes God takes them. And in those moments, we realize that everything we've done in their lives to that point has renewed meaning.

Why was it important that I preached to that person? Because this day was coming. Why was it important that I counseled that person? Because this day was coming. Why was it important that I evangelized that person? Because this day was coming. Why was it important that I held that person's hand? Because this day was coming. Why was it important that I did all the things I did with that person, and with all the rest of these people? Because this day is coming for all of us. We are preparing people to meet God. Entertainment doesn't do that. Coddling doesn't do that. The gospel does that. And when we grasp that, it changes the magnitude and gravitas of the ministry we have.

Finally, our labor gives us hope. You know there's a huge difference between standing over a ninety-year-old man, preaching a funeral for people who are nodding and smiling because that old saint lived a full life of loving and serving the Lord, and standing over a casket two feet long. How, without the hope of the resurrection, can you look into the eyes of parents who only had a few moments with their child? How do you preach to a husband and five young children after a forty-two-year-old mother who went into the hospital because she felt bad was dead from an infection a few days later? You better not try to reason your way out of that one.

The Resurrection Transforms Everything

Because the hope of the gospel and the resurrection changes our anthropology, the reality that this is not our home, the reality that we are being prepared for something more, and the reality of the resurrection of Christ change how we think about these people who have passed from this life before us. Because the resurrection changes our soteriology, we think differently about what Christ has done for them and for us. Because it changes our missiology, we think differently about how we utilize that moment and what we say and why we say it. And now we know our labor is not in vain.

This is why the doctrine of the resurrection is so important. This is why it wasn't enough for Paul to just win the argument. This is why it wasn't enough to have people just confess, "Okay, I believe it's a possibility." No! That's not enough. This is your life. This is who you are. This is the way you understand yourself as a human being and the way you understand every other human being. It changes what you mean by justification and adoption and sanctification and glorification, and it changes how you live—what you do in gospel ministry and in righteous living.

Everything is changed when we understand the resurrection of Jesus Christ. And this is why we stand over those elements time and time again and remind our people time and time again that whenever we eat this bread and drink this cup, we proclaim the Lord's death until he comes. We must always be resurrection-centered. Why? Because there is no gospel without the resurrection. Therefore, if we're not resurrection-centered, we're not gospel-centered.

7

LIVING IN THE HOPE OF
LIBERATION FROM BONDAGE

Romans 8:16–25

J. LIGON DUNCAN III

In Romans 6–8, Paul speaks to the issue of how grace reigns in righteousness in our lives. Romans 8 deals with the role of the Holy Spirit in the life of the believer, and Paul addresses nine exceedingly practical questions about day-to-day Christian living:

1. How are we able to grow in grace despite our indwelling sin (8:1–4)?
2. How can we tell the difference between godliness and worldliness (8:5–11)?
3. How does the Holy Spirit show us that we are children of God (8:12–17)?
4. How do our present sufferings work for future glory (8:18–25)?
5. How does the Holy Spirit intercede for us (8:26–27)?
6. How can we be certain that God's promises to us will be fulfilled (8:28–30)?
7. How much is God for us (8:31–32)?

8. How secure are we in God's justification of us (8:33–34)?

9. How can we be more than conquerors (8:35–39)?

All of these things are as practical for the Christian life today as they were for the Roman Christians who heard these words read and preached to them.

Present Suffering and Future Glory Linked Together

In Romans 8:16–25, the passage examined in this chapter, Paul gives his answers to the third and fourth questions. This is a passage about present suffering and future glory, two things that are integrally connected. Our present suffering is neither incidental to our future glory nor accidental to our present Christian life. Instead, it is purposeful and deeply connected to our sonship now and glory later.

Before proceeding, we must understand that the picture of the end that God paints for us in Scripture (otherwise known as eschatology) has aspects of both "now" and "not yet." Most of us understand that. Some, however, have critiqued evangelical eschatology by claiming that evangelicals care so much about the "not yet" that they do not adequately care about the "now." Evangelicals, they contend, have been so concerned about the salvation of people that they have missed the big picture of the new heaven and the new earth, of which our salvation is only a small part. Each of us is just another brick in the wall, and there is something much bigger than us.

On the contrary, we affirm that both "now" and "not yet" matter. The "not yet" matters now and the "now" matters in the "not yet." This idea is not new; the Bible unequivocally teaches that right now counts forever and forever counts right now, and Christians have understood this for a long time. Paul pulls all that together for us in Romans 8:16–25.

Thinking about Your Suffering

Beginning in Romans 8:16–17, Paul tells us that the witness of the Spirit assures us of our sonship amid our present suffering.

"The Spirit himself bears witness with our spirit that we are children of God, and if children, then heirs—heirs of God and fellow heirs with Christ, provided we suffer with him in order that we may also be glorified with him." Christians are assured that they are children of God by the witness of the Spirit. The Spirit himself witnesses to your spirit that you are a joint heir with Jesus Christ!

But do you sometimes wish Paul had just left out the final words of verse 17? It's similar to Philippians 1:29, where he says, "For it has been granted to you that for the sake of Christ you should not only believe in him but also suffer for his sake." The first part sounds great, but why couldn't Paul leave off that bit about suffering? It is indeed a great gift to believe in the Lord Jesus Christ, but it's also a great gift to suffer for his sake. The same principle applies in Romans 8:16, because Paul teaches there that our suffering also bears witness that we are the children of God. Far from being incidental to our experience, accidental in the Christian life, or outside of God's purposes, our suffering is a witness to us that we are the children of God.

Notice how Paul speaks of assurance as neither totally objective nor totally subjective, but both. In other words, there are internal and external aspects to assurance. But Paul also plainly teaches that it is the Holy Spirit who gives assurance, not anyone else. None of us can give people assurance. Remember that in your evangelism. We can never replace the witness of the Spirit.

Paul's characteristic emphasis on suffering is also evident in these verses because, as will be seen in the remainder of the passage, having the witness of the Spirit does not mean you will not suffer. God had one Son without sin, but no sons without suffering. If one is to live the Christian life, Paul explains, he or she must know that in advance.

How do you think about your suffering? Do you try and cope with it by ignoring it? Do you bite your lip and keep a strong outward face? Has it made you bitter or even angry at God? Has it made you feel hopeless, or do you just feel numb? Paul knows it is vital for us as children of God to have right views of suffering, trial, and tribulation because they are part of God's purposes for our future glory. Those who blame suffering, pain, and poverty on your lack of faith fail to understand what Paul is teaching here. Those who say that even God is surprised by your suffering do not begin to understand God's wonderful purposes in the suffering we experience in this life.

"We are children of God, and if children, then heirs," Paul says; but what does that mean? Of what, exactly, are we heirs? We are heirs of all the Abrahamic promises. If you are a believer in the Lord Jesus Christ, you are inheritors of the Abrahamic promise. All of the promises of God to Abraham are yours.

A Greater Inheritance

But it's not mere things that God will give you. He will give you the greatest inheritance in the Abrahamic promise: God himself. "I will be your God, and you will be my people." So what does the Christian get in his or her inheritance? God! God *is* our inheritance. And Paul doesn't stop there. He calls us "fellow heirs with Christ" (Rom. 8:17). What belongs to Jesus is yours because you belong to him.

Four Aspects of This Suffering and Glory

Paul elaborates on his main lesson with four points in Romans 8:18–25.

Suffering Now

In verse 18, he speaks of "the sufferings of this present time." In other words, although the Spirit witnesses to your spirit that you are a child of God, that you are filled with the Holy Spirit, that you are a godly follower of the Lord Jesus Christ, that you were redeemed, called, justified, and adopted, you are not guaranteed a life of painless bliss. In fact, you are guaranteed a life of suffering, partly because we live in a fallen world where pain is unavoidable. At the same time, it is precisely because we are truly children of God that we suffer, inwardly and outwardly.

I don't know how many times I've learned, forgotten, and learned again that lesson in my Christian life. Suffering will catch me unaware, and I throw up my hands and say, "Something is not right here. This is not how it is supposed to be!" But Paul teaches us that our suffering is the consequence of being a new creation in this old creation, and God in his sovereignty has a purpose for our suffering that transcends "now" and stretches into the "not yet."

A verse from a hymn written by Margaret Clarkson begins,

O Father, you are sovereign,
the Lord of human pain.[1]

Sovereign Father, says Clarkson, you're not just the God of blessings who has nothing to do with my pain; you're the Lord even of my pain. God can make even suffering serve his eternal interests in us and produce a weight of glory beyond all comparison.

GLORY LATER

In Romans 8:18, Paul also begins to point us to the future. "I consider that the sufferings of this present time," he says, "are not worth comparing with the glory that is to be revealed to us." Paul says our trials here are real—and sometimes they are so real and overwhelming that it seems they are beyond our endurance, so that we feel like Job and regret our birth. But Paul explains that even if we count up all the suffering we go through, it cannot compare to the glory that is going to be revealed to us. The glory of the "not yet" is put before our eyes now, not so that we can escape and sing, "Pie in the sky, by

---

1. Margaret Clarkson, "O Father, You Are Sovereign," 1980.

and by." No, it is put before us so we can be strengthened to endure, engage, and bless.

When Paul says, "the sufferings of this present time," know that he includes both the inward battle with sin and the outward battle with the fallen world and the suffering it brings. Nonetheless, all the suffering brought to us by inward and outward battles cannot begin to compare to the glory that is to come. Paul is saying that God uses those sufferings to produce the future glory that he will reveal to you and in you.

God is going to make you so much like Jesus Christ that if you were to meet your glorified self now, you would be tempted to fall down and worship, as John was tempted to worship the angel in Revelation. The glory that he is producing in you outweighs the suffering, because through suffering you will be made like Jesus.

In *The Lord of the Rings*, Aragorn dies after a long and magnificent reign as king. Tolkien says of his body:

> Then a great beauty was revealed in him, so that all who after came there looked on him in wonder; for they saw that the grace of his youth, and the valour of his manhood, and the wisdom and majesty of his age were blended together. And long there he lay, an image of the Kings of Men in glory undimmed before the breaking of the world.[2]

Understand that quite the same thing will happen to you, but you're going to be alive! One day, we'll meet one another in heaven and say, "Perfect!" We see in part how God works in us now and admire his work in each other, but on that day we will be amazed by the perfection that God gives us. In the garden, the Serpent basically said to Adam and Eve, "Take that fruit and you'll be like God." Adam and Eve should have replied, "What do you mean we will be like God? We *are* like God! We are created in the image and likeness of God."

---

2. J. R. R. Tolkien, *The Return of the King: Being the Third Part of the Lord of the Rings* (New York: Ballantine, 1955), 378.

But they took the fruit. Far from Satan's promise, they became less like God. His image in humanity, though not erased, was deeply marred. In our redemption, however, God pardons and accepts us, and begins a process of remaking us into the fullness of his image. One day he will look at us and we will be like him, or as John puts it, "We shall be like him, because we shall see him as he is" (1 John 3:2). God is making you like him even (and especially) in your suffering.

Are you surprised by that? If your Savior learned obedience through what he suffered (Heb. 5:8), did you think it was going to be different for you? Do you think God was up to something in his Son? Of course he was! Do you think God is up to something in you, son or daughter of God? Yes, he is. The apostle Paul says that you cannot possibly look at the present suffering without looking at the future glory. God is up to something in you. He is making you like him.

CREATION RESTORED

Look at Romans 8:19–21. The whole of the nonhuman universe is caught up in the plight of the fall and this hope of future glory. The apostle Paul says:

> For the creation waits with eager longing for the revealing of the sons of God. For the creation was subjected to futility, not willingly, but because of him who subjected it, in hope that the creation itself will be set free from its bondage to corruption and obtain the freedom of the glory of the children of God.

Genesis 3 tells us there were consequences for the creation in the fall of Adam. The vanity spoken of by the Preacher in Ecclesiastes applies not just to us but also to the creation. The creation suffers from that futility.

As you look at your own suffering, Paul says, realize that even the creation is frustrated. You're not alone in this old creation that longs for the new creation. You're not alone in this old heaven and earth looking forward to the new. The creation itself "has been groaning together in the pains of childbirth until now" (Rom. 8:22).

Spotlight on creation? But running with Paul's words on the creation, some say that evangelicals have overemphasized individual justification and eschatology and forgotten the new creation, when in fact the important part is the new creation. The proponents of this idea say that we are just a part of that new creation. Look at verse 19 again: what is the creation waiting for? "The creation waits with eager longing for the revealing of the sons of God." The new creation is waiting for you.

Tom Schreiner replies:

> We should note that creation, even though it is the subject of these verses, does not constitute the center stage of Paul's vision. What creation longs for is the eschatological unveiling of the children of God. The focus is not finally on the transformation of the created world, although that is included, but the future redemption that awaits God's children.[3]

The unveiling of God's church. When God one day gives a great display of his glory by unveiling his people, the church, as his grand design, the creation will gasp, "Wow!" After all, what is creation created to do but declare the glory of God (Psalm 19)? And when God displays his redeemed people, creation will do exactly that, singing, "Look at what he did!" Paul exhorts us to never forget that one day the creation is going to be amazed at what God has done for us and in us.

A LIFE OF ENDURANCE

In Romans 8:23–25, Paul explains that in light of these facts, we must live purposefully, persevering now in our pain, suffering,

---

3. Thomas R. Schreiner, *Romans*, Baker Exegetical Commentary on the New Testament (Grand Rapids, MI: Baker, 1998), 430.

and futility, in a confident anticipation of this future glory. "And not only the creation," he says, "but we ourselves, who have the firstfruits of the Spirit, groan inwardly as we wait eagerly for adoption as sons, the redemption of our bodies" (8:23). But hold on a second! Didn't Paul just tell us in verse 16 that the Spirit witnesses that we are children of God? What then does he mean by saying that we wait for our adoption? If we are already children, what are we waiting for?

We await the redemption of the body. Our future hope is not the intermediate state, where we will be absent from the body but present with the Lord, as precious as that truth is. That is not the blessed hope. The blessed hope, if I can use the language of Job, is this:

> After my skin has been thus destroyed,
>> yet in my flesh I shall see God. (Job 19:26)

God will redeem our corruptible bodies and make them incorruptible, and we will be formed in the fullness of what he created humans to be. Then our adoption will be vindicated, displayed, and declared to the entire universe. The murderers of martyrs will see the glorified bodies of their Christian victims remade and will hear God declare, "These are my children." On that day, the haters of God and his people will tremble at God's vindication of his adopted and redeemed people.

Brothers and sisters, we must look to that future hope, regardless of what suffering we experience now in our bodies. "For who hopes for what he sees? But if we hope for what we do not see, we wait for it with patience" (Rom. 8:24–25).

Paul stresses that the Christian life is fundamentally a life of endurance. Though we may experience a foretaste of these promises, we will never see their complete fulfillment in this life. Therefore, we must live in hope. If we focus exclusively on the "now," we will fail to live in it. But if our eyes are on what God will do in the "not yet," that will enable us to live in the "now" and to endure until the "not yet."

Endurance and perseverance are often underestimated. But as Tom Cannon, coordinator for Reformed University Fellowship, wrote to several campus ministers, "Endurance trumps zeal every time." That's good advice for all Christians, but especially ministers. Romans 8:16–25 tells us how to endure. We must set our eyes on that future hope.

Now and Then

But if our hope is on the future, won't we ignore the "now"? Let me answer with something provocative. The Reformed doctrine of justification ended chattel slavery in the British Empire. Some argue that the doctrine of justification is too individualistic, future-focused, and asocial; it ought to be modified to make it more social so that it speaks to the "now" and our engagement in this world. No, it was the doctrine of justification as the Protestant Reformers expounded it that led John Newton and William Wilberforce to spend their last breaths to set slaves free. They understood this passage.

You can't live now unless your hope is on the "not yet." The "now" is so overwhelming that we can't survive without the hope of the "not yet," so Paul teaches us to suffer and endure to the glory of God by pointing us to the future, and especially what we will be then.

Stephen Marshall, one of the members of the Westminster Assembly of Divines, said this concerning what God is going to do as he builds his church through suffering:

> All the glory that [God] looks for to eternity must arise out of this one work of building Zion; this one work shall be the only monument of his glory to eternity: this goodly world, this heaven and earth, that you see and enjoy the use of, is set up only as a shop, as a workshop, to stand only for a week, for [a few] thousand years . . . and when his work is done he will throw

this piece of clay down again, and out of this he looks for no other glory . . . but this piece [his church, his people] he sets up for a higher end, to be the eternal mansion of his holiness and honour; this is his *metropolis*, his temple, his house.[4]

What God is building is you like you were meant to be—only better.

4. C. H. Spurgeon, *The Treasury of David*, 3 vols. in one (Peabody, MA: Hendrickson, 1988), 2:266.

8

A NEW HEAVEN AND A NEW EARTH

Revelation 21:1–22:5

PHILIP GRAHAM RYKEN

Admittedly, Revelation is not the easiest book in the Bible. My favorite comment comes from Ambrose Bierce, who defined Revelation as the book "in which Saint John the Divine concealed all that he knew. The revealing is done by the commentators, who know nothing."[1] Yet as puzzling as Revelation can be, in its final chapters we find a sanctuary for the heart of every lonely pilgrim who is longing for home.

Longing for Home

Do you ever have moments when you catch a little glimpse of what it would be like to live in perfect communion with Christ—in a place of joy and wholeness and peace?

My first eschatological experience took place in the backyard of our family home in Wheaton, Illinois, on a warm afternoon in the springtime when our backyard became the neighborhood baseball diamond. The garage on one side was the backstop, and the white picket fence to the neighbor's yard was for home runs.

---

1. Ambrose Bierce, *The Devil's Dictionary* (New York: Dover, 1993), 107.

As the children began to play, the adults doing yard work gradually drifted over, and soon all of us were playing together. It was my first baseball game. Much later in life, when I read Zechariah's prophecy about the New Jerusalem filled with the sounds of children playing there (Zech. 8:5), I could think back to my first childhood baseball game and recognize that it had pointed me home.

The mother of a special needs child testifies to a very different eschatological experience. Her teenage son is largely confined to a specialized wheelchair. Sometimes she describes what it was like for their family to visit a ski slope where her son could go up the mountain with a ski instructor who had a chair for disabled skiers. When she looked over at the ski lodge and saw a row of empty wheelchairs, she knew that the people who usually sat in them had been freed of their limitations and were up on the mountain, enjoying God's creation. Tears streamed down her face as she longed for a home beyond all brokenness and pain.

Or consider the dying words of D. L. Moody. The famous evangelist was in his last hours; all day he hovered between heaven and earth. Moody told the people at his bedside that God was calling him home and that he was beginning to see the glory: "I have been beyond the gates of death; I have been to the very portals of heaven." Sadly, the family had lost two young grandchildren. So we can imagine how deeply touched they all were when Moody suddenly cried out, "Dwight! Irene!—I see the children's faces!"[2]

What experience has awakened your longing for home? For many Christians, a longing for heaven comes during times of painful loss, severe trial, and unrelenting suffering. Once I shared a long list of trials and difficulties with other Christian college presidents and their spouses. Some of my struggles were institutional, others personal; and it got to the point where people started to laugh because it sounded like more than one person should have

---

2. William Revell Moody, *D. L. Moody* (New York: Macmillan, 1930), 537–38.

to suffer all at once. At the end of my litany of woe, I had one final sentence that I wanted to speak to my friends. My heart was so full of emotion that it took me about two minutes to get it out. What I wanted to say—reflecting especially on the sufferings of our family—was simply this: "All I want is to see my children safely home."

That is what this chapter is about. It is about looking forward to the home that God has for his people—the home we glimpse in times of joy and long for in times of pain and suffering. We are longing for the place where there will be no more "not yet," but only an eternal "now"—the place that John described in Revelation 21 and 22.

Creation Recapitulated

My purpose in expounding the last two chapters of the Bible is to awaken greater homesickness, as well as renewed hope, so that everyone who reads these words may go out into the world like the apostles, the abolitionists, and all the other great men and women of God who had such a vision of glory that they were able to do the suffering work of the church in the world until Jesus comes again.

What is so amazing about Revelation 21 and 22 is the way that seemingly every strand of Scripture is drawn together and brought to its perfect conclusion. The book of Revelation contains roughly five hundred allusions to or quotations from the Old Testament. In the last two chapters, every major theme from Scripture reappears. Covenant, atonement, temple, and kingdom are all here. The Father, the Son, and the Spirit are here, of course. Jesus Christ is here in his prophetic, priestly, and kingly offices. We see heaven and earth, sin and salvation, creation and consummation. It is all here in these last two chapters.

It is characteristic of any great work of literature to have in its ending something that brings a sense of harmony to the whole. Like the finale of a symphony, or the confetti at the end of a national championship, or even just the last bite of a delicious dessert, there is a satisfying conclusion. This is most perfectly true here at the closing of the canon of Scripture. The Bible is the great tapestry of God's work in history, and all of its threads are bound together at the end of Revelation.

As we come to this great ending and tie together all the loose threads, notice first that creation will be recapitulated. Revelation 21 and 22 are filled with echoes from Eden. Again, this is characteristic of great literature. There is a sense of coming back home. It's like *The Hobbit* and *The Lord of the Rings*, by J. R. R. Tolkien, which begin in the Shire. The protagonists leave their home to have all kinds of adventures, with elves and dwarves, and dungeons and dragons. But at the end of it all, they come back home to the Shire.

Or, to give another example from literature, consider the poem "East Coker," by T. S. Eliot. Eliot begins with the line "In my beginning is my end," and when we get to the end of the poem, he says, "In my end is my beginning." Readers have a sense of traversing a distance, but also of coming back home again, so there is a sense of harmony and completion.

BOOKENDS OF HISTORY

We get the same feeling when we turn to the first verse of Revelation 21 and read about "a new heaven and a new earth." The verse that comes immediately to mind is the very first verse in all of Scripture: "In the beginning, God created the heavens and the earth" (Gen. 1:1). A literary scholar would call this kind of repetition an inclusio. Genesis and Revelation form the inclusio of all inclusios: the grand story of God's redemption begins and ends with a creation of heaven and earth.

In Revelation 21:2 we meet a bride and groom. This also reminds us of Eden, where a woman (Eve) was presented to a man (Adam), and the two became husband and wife. Suddenly the man burst into poetry, singing the world's first love song:

. . . bone of my bones
   and flesh of my flesh. (Gen. 2:23)

Then, in Revelation 21:3, God walks into the picture. He is there with the bride and groom in their happy home. So it was in the very beginning, in the early chapters of Genesis, when God would come and walk with his people in the cool of the day (Gen. 3:8).

As we read further down in the chapter, we find reference to the sun and the moon. Not that there is any sun or moon in the glorious city of God, of course—yet they are mentioned here to provide context. Somehow this seems appropriate. The Bible is bringing to mind the beginning of the world, when God called all things into being and put two great lights in the sky to rule the day and the night.

When we turn to Revelation 22, we find that a river runs through it: "the river of the water of life" (22:1). There was a river in Eden, too, for in Genesis we read about "a river flowing out of Eden to water the garden," which "divided and became four rivers" (Gen. 2:10). And what do we see at the center of the new heaven and the new earth? A tree of life yielding fruit. If there is anything we associate with the garden of Eden, it is the tree that God planted in its center for the blessing of humanity.

As we walk through Revelation 21 and 22, surveying the new heaven and the new earth, we find ourselves saying, "There is something familiar about this place; I feel like I've been here before." Heaven is a domicile with a sense of déjà vu. It is creation recapitulated.

This is in keeping both with our nature as human beings and with the character of God. It is in keeping with our humanity because creation is our once-and-future home. When we reach the new heaven and the new earth, we will not feel dislocated but will find that we are in the place where we have always belonged.

THE PLACE WE HAVE ALWAYS BELONGED

There is a deep longing in every human heart to return to our ancestral home. Crosby, Stills, Nash, and Young sing about this in their song "Woodstock": "We got to get ourselves back to the garden." This is part of God's purpose for his people: a return to the place where we began. It is a place of relationship between man and woman and fellowship with God—a place of light and life, of trees and water. This is the home where we have always belonged, and always will. In the words of Chad Walsh, a literary critic who came to faith in Christ through the witness of C. S. Lewis, "I believe man once lived in utopia, but does no longer, and that he is always trying to return. The name of his first utopia was Eden. . . . It is a part of our heritage. We want to go back. . . . We are haunted by memories of the original garden. . . . We are Displaced Persons, but our old homeland burns and glows in our hearts."[3]

Coming back to our old homeland is in keeping not only with our human nature but also with the character of God, who always finishes what he starts. He is "the Alpha and the Omega, the beginning and the end" (Rev. 21:6). What other God could work such a perfect plan—bringing the Bible to such a fitting conclusion and the plan of salvation to such a magnificent culmination—except the God who has been there since before time began and who sees the end from the beginning? It is because God was always there that we find our end in our beginning, and our beginning in our end.

The Curse Reversed

When creation is recapitulated, the curse will be reversed. We are no longer living in Paradise; our address is somewhere east of Eden. Humanity has fallen into sin and therefore has come under judgment. When Adam and Eve ate the forbidden fruit, they were

---

3. Chad Walsh, *From Utopia to Nightmare* (London: Bles, 1962), 30.

banished from the garden. This was partly an act of grace, as God was waiting for the second Adam to bring salvation, but it is an exile nonetheless. Our great sin has brought endless woe on the human race: guilt, alienation, slavery, warfare, abuse.

Our blessed race has been cursed because of all this sin. Every new day brings news of our desperation. We see racial strife in cities across the United States. As we look around the world, we lament the plight of a persecuted church. What a grief it was to learn in the spring of 2015 that in northern Iraq, in the city of Mosul, where for the last fifteen hundred years people have been worshiping God in the name of Jesus Christ, the bells of the churches were silent for the first time on Easter because Christians had been driven away from their homes. In Iraq and elsewhere, many people have lost their lives. Whether this has been because of ISIS, which has been deliberate in saying that it has a message of death for the nation of the cross, or whether it is because of Boko Haram, which has attacked students in Nigeria, Christians and others are being killed for their faith. These are only some of the burdens we bear in a fallen world.

But when we peek at the last pages of the Bible, we see how the story will end. The dreadful consequences of sin in a fallen world will be overcome; the curse will be reversed. Thus Revelation 21 and 22 are full of images from Scripture of things that have been damaged and all but destroyed by sin, but one day will be restored.

We see this already in the first verse of chapter 21, where John tells us that "the sea was no more." This is significant theologically because in the Old Testament the sea generally is depicted as a place of chaos and danger. The sea represents everything that chafes and frets under the dominion of God; everything that is out of our control. But there is nothing like that in the new heaven and the new earth. Everything there is under the orderly blessing of God.

Then notice the way Revelation describes the city of Jerusalem: it is called "the holy city" (21:2) With these words, another curse is reversed. For if ever there was a city that was *un*holy, a city that turned its back on God and fell under his judgment, it was the city of Jerusalem. Remember how devastated the city was in the days of Jeremiah, when women and children were dead in the streets. Jeremiah's Jerusalem was as ruined as any city in the history of the world. Remember too the curses of the prophets, who said Jerusalem would become a ruin, a haunt for jackals (Isa. 34:13). Think of the distress of our Lord, as reflected in the words of his lament: "O Jerusalem, Jerusalem, the city that kills the prophets. . . . How often would I have gathered your children together as a hen gathers her brood under her wings, and you were not willing!" (Matt. 23:37). Yet here in Revelation, Jerusalem is called "the holy city." The sins of God's people have been forgiven; their iniquities have been pardoned; the curse has been reversed.

Marriage Failed, Marriage Restored

We see something similar in the beautiful image of the "bride adorned for her husband" (Rev. 21:2). The bride is another familiar image from Scripture, going all the way back to our first parents in the garden of Eden. All through the Old Testament this image is applied to the relationship God has with his people. "Your Maker is your husband," the prophet says (Isa. 54:5).

Yet this image mainly occurs when the Bible is recording a litany of marital failure. This sad theme comes to a critical point in Jeremiah 2, where God files for divorce. The prophet records a covenant lawsuit on the grounds of spiritual adultery. God shows up in divorce court to provide evidence upon evidence of marital failure. Or think of Hosea, who was called to marry Gomer, a prostitute, as a sign of Israel's spiritual infidelity. Tim Keller puts the whole Old Testament story into perspective when he says that God has been trapped in the longest bad marriage in history.

But when we get to the end of Scripture, the curse is reversed. It's a wedding scene. The people of God are "prepared as a bride adorned for her husband." What makes this especially remarkable is that the groom paid the dowry with his own blood. He did it in such a way that everything that was stained and sinful in his bride, the church, has now been made spotless and clean and perfect. Every bride takes great pains to make sure she is perfect for her wedding. I've performed about a hundred weddings, and I've never seen a bride who is anything but beautiful. Revelation uses this picture of pure white holiness to show us sin forgiven, iniquity pardoned, and therefore the curse reversed.

No More Tears

Then we come to a remarkable promise: "He will wipe away every tear from their eyes" (Rev. 21:4). No death. No mourning. No crying. All of that has passed away.

It's a beautiful image—God wiping away our tears. I imagine that when we arrive in heaven there will still be a tear or two on our cheeks from the sufferings of this earthly life. But God will be there with the handkerchief of his grace to say, "There, there, my child." Then he will wipe away every last tear. How many tears we shed in this life! We have tears of sorrow of repentance for sin, of grief over the loss of people we love, of regret for lost opportunities, of frustration, and of anger. Anyone sensitive to pain has many tears. But here is a promise we can hardly imagine in this fallen world: no more tears!

The Death of Death

And no more death! The last enemy (1 Cor. 15:26)—maybe the greatest enemy—has also been destroyed. Death brings many pains and frustrations. We see this clearly in the emotions of Jesus Christ at the tomb of Lazarus, when he wept, seemingly uncontrollably. If we understand the vocabulary words in this passage properly, our Lord was full of righteous indignation for what death had brought to the human race (see John 11:35). We have all experienced it: the terrible finality of the death of someone we love who cannot be brought back to life in this world. But one day that curse will be reversed. Death will find its death in the death of Christ, and life will come to life in his resurrection from the grave.

To put this promise into perspective, consider the testimony of Roger Lundin, who taught English at Wheaton College until his death in 2015. Dr. Lundin sometimes would describe the disturbing nightmares he had as a teenager in the weeks and months after the death of his brother. The two of them had shared a room, with their beds on opposite walls. Lundin had a recurring dream that his beloved brother was in his usual place, except that life had passed from his mortal body. In the dream someone would tell him that if only he could reach out and touch the body, his brother would spring back to life and be restored to his family. But of course, for one reason or another, Lundin would always fail to make the life-giving connection. So he would wake up in a cold sweat, feeling guilty for his failure. Then he would look over at the empty bed and experience the desolation of his loss all over again.

Dr. Lundin's sad experience reminds us of the extraordinary story that Luke tells about the time when Jesus reached out and touched a dead man's bed (Luke 7:11–17). The Savior was traveling to a town called Nain, and as he came near the gates, he met a funeral procession. A widow's only young son had died, and the whole town had gathered to carry his body out for burial. But when Jesus reached out to touch the dead man's bed, death itself was stopped in its tracks. A single touch, one word of command, and the dead man came back to life!

Jesus Christ has authority over life and death. By the power of his resurrection, he will never die again. And by that same power, he will raise every one of his followers to eternal life. Jesus was only the first to rise. His plan is for all his children to rise, and never to die again. No more death! The death of Christ is the death of death, and his resurrection is the birth of eternal life.

No More Pain

No more death, and also no more pain. This too will be taken away. Some pains can feel even worse than death: broken relationships, separation, divorce, rejection, chronic illness, words spoken in anger or hatred that we will never forget. Ligon Duncan mentioned Margaret Clarkson in the previous chapter, and what he said was true: the gifted hymn writer suffered chronic arthritic pain from early childhood all through life. This personal experience was part of the background for the dramatic proclamation in one of her hymns that Jesus Christ is "the Lord of human pain."[4] Sometimes the pains of life are so great that we can hardly bear them. They are all part of the curse of creation itself groaning under the pain of sin (see Rom. 8:22). But one day that curse will be reversed!

No More Sin

None of these things will be present in the permanent home God is making for his people: no pain or crying or death. Furthermore, the destruction of death will be the end of sin. Praise God! Revelation refers to "the cowardly, the faithless, the detestable" (21:8), and then it lists many other sins that appear in the worst vice lists in the New Testament. What Revelation says about these sins is that none of them will be present in the new heaven and the new earth: "But nothing unclean will ever enter it, nor anyone who does what is detestable or false, but only those who are written in the Lamb's book of life" (21:27). In one sense, this is a fearful verse, because it pronounces everlasting doom on all the enemies of God. Anyone who has not repented of sin has no place in God's everlasting home. But this warning is given to us in grace. All we need to say is "I don't want to be a sinner. I want to turn away from sin. I want to be cleansed of my sin. Jesus, I want the forgiveness that you have to offer."

---

4. Margaret Clarkson, "O Father, You Are Sovereign," 1980.

As we come to God for the forgiveness of our sins in the name of Jesus, Revelation 21:27 is a hopeful promise because it shows God's absolute triumph over evil. There is no sin in glory. Is any reverse of the curse greater than an end to all our iniquity? We struggle with sin all our lives. But as the great theologian Augustine considered the human heart, he looked forward to the happy day when we would not be able to sin. One day we will be delivered from the sin that so easily entangles us. What we do and what we want to do will be one and the same. By the life-giving grace of Jesus Christ, we will reach a state of sinless perfection.

As a young woman, Joni Eareckson (Tada) was crippled in a diving accident. Afterward, she came to Christ and devoted her life to serving people with disabilities. Given her acute physical limitations, her deepest longing for eternity may come as a surprise:

> I can't wait to be clothed in righteousness, without a trace of sin. Yes, it will be wonderful to stand, stretch, and reach to the sky. But it will be more wonderful to offer praise that is pure and won't be crippled by distractions, disabled by insincerity, handicapped by a ho-hum half-heartedness. Now my joy will join with yours, and we will bubble over with effervescent adoration, finally able to worship with the Father and the Son. For me, this is the best part of heaven.[5]

WE WILL BE ENTIRELY SANCTIFIED AND SATISFIED

But there is more: not just sinlessness, but also satisfaction. Can we even conceive of this? Of all the cursed things we suffer in this fallen world, our underlying discontent is one of the worst. Life never measures up to our expectations. Even at the best of times, some little disappointment gets in the way of total happiness.

I remember a moment like this at the shoe store. Sadly, I had lost my favorite pair of Top-Siders. I looked everywhere, but they were nowhere to be found. Not even my mother could find them.

---

5. Joni Eareckson Tada, *Heaven—Your Real Home* (Grand Rapids, MI: Zondervan, 1995), 41.

So I went to the Sperry store to get the exact same style, only to discover that they didn't make that kind anymore. I was grumpy because I couldn't get the shoes I wanted—until I remembered that I had been in the Dominican Republic just a few weeks before. While I was there my sneaker fell apart, but fortunately someone was able to glue it back together. Suddenly I realized that the reason he knew how to glue it back together was that he had done the same thing for hundreds of children in that community—children who felt lucky to have even one pair of shoes. How quickly and unreasonably we become discontent!

Gregg Easterbrook wrote about this in a 2003 book called *The Progress Paradox*.[6] Easterbrook's subtitle was *How Life Gets Better While People Feel Worse*. He describes how affluent we have become—better food, better healthcare, better education, better communication, better climate control, better entertainment, better transportation—all of that. Yet, when sociologists do their surveys, and people in America indicate where they fall on the satisfaction scale, they are only "slightly satisfied."

Easterbrook has many explanations for this paradox—a condition some have termed *affluenza*—but the fundamental problem is that this fallen world cannot satisfy anyone. What we really need, and what we are really looking for, whether we know it or not, is a relationship with the living God. David expressed it well when he said,

> My soul thirsts for you;
> my flesh faints for you,
>> as in a dry and weary land where there is no water.
>> (Ps. 63:1)

When we come to the end of Revelation and read the last chapter in the story of our salvation, our thirst is finally satisfied. Jesus says, "To the thirsty I will give from the spring of the water of

---

6. Gregg Easterbrook, *The Progress Paradox: How Life Gets Better While People Feel Worse* (New York: Random House, 2003).

life" (Rev. 21:6). This is an image of satisfaction. Jesus is not just describing heaven's water supply. He is talking about the spiritual contentment that only the living God can provide. In the kingdom to come there will be a whole river of the water of life (Rev. 22:1). This is another great theme from Scripture. Think of the man who is like a tree planted by streams of water in Psalm 1, or the river that runs through the city of God in Psalm 46, or the extraordinary tributary that flows from the throne of God in Ezekiel, with the power to freshen salty seas (Ezek. 47:8). Think especially of the promises of Jesus Christ: that he would give "living water" (John 4:10); and "Whoever believes in me, as the Scripture has said, 'Out of his heart will flow rivers of living water'" (John 7:38). These promises of satisfaction will be fulfilled when we come home to the kingdom of God.

There is much more we could say about the reversal of the curse. Today we see nations at war, but in Revelation we see the healing of all nations. Every people, tongue, and tribe will come to him. All of the old hostilities will end, every sworn enemy will be reconciled, and the peoples of the earth will be healed into total harmony.

Revelation gathers all of these promises together in a single verse and says, "No longer will there be anything accursed" (Rev. 22:3). A great change will take place—a total reversal. Whether we are talking about marriage, the city, physical pain, death, broken relationships, or international conflicts—anything that is wounded in this fallen world—the curse will be reversed.

Salvation Consummated

But wait: there's more! God's plan is not simply to take us back somewhere. He does not intend simply to unwind or rewind something. He wants to carry things forward to absolute perfection. So here is a third great theme in the last two chapters of Scripture: salvation consummated. God will bring everything to the perfect conclusion he always intended—something way above and far beyond anything we've ever seen before.

ALL THINGS NEW

Notice how often the word "new" comes up, especially at the beginning of Revelation 21. "New heaven." "New earth." The promise is not just being taken away from earth to heaven; it's a new earth as well as a new heaven. God will not simply take us out of this world into another world, but he will make this world new. And how new it will be! There will be a new heaven—a new wilderness tabernacle of sorts, a new kind of temple—with the coming of the New Jerusalem. When God descended to visit Israel's tabernacle and temple, he was dwelling with his people and filling the sanctuary with his glory.

THE FULLNESS OF HIS SANCTUARY

Given this background, in which the worship of God's people was always centered at a physical structure, we would expect some sort of temple within the New Jerusalem—some particular place for the worship of God. But here is the big surprise: there is no temple! A temple is a dwelling place for God. But here the whole blessed metropolis is a dwelling place for God. The entire urban community is a sanctuary: every street, every alleyway, every nook and cranny of every building is filled with the light of God's presence. It is *all* a temple.

This is the consummation of the temple theme from Scripture. When Moses built the tabernacle and when Solomon built the temple, God came down from heaven to live with his people. But one day God will come to be with us forever. When that day comes, there will be no temple because the whole beautiful place will be filled with the glorious splendor of the radiant majesty of God. We will see the consummation of the salvation promise of the presence of God.

Christ Enthroned

Of all the glories of heaven, this will be the greatest by far: the glory of God himself. So consider Christ enthroned. Revelation 21 and

22 are not about a place, primarily, but about a person. Yes, when salvation is consummated, then creation will be recapitulated and the curse reversed. But at the center of it all will be the person of Jesus Christ, whose presence will make heaven to be heaven.

Jesus is everywhere in these two chapters as his presence pervades the city of the New Jerusalem and his glory suffuses the atmosphere of the new heaven and the new earth. Indeed, this is why they are so glorious. In Revelation 21:2 Jesus is the husband waiting eagerly to see the beauty of his bride. In verse 3 he is the voice speaking from the throne and pronouncing the fulfillment of God's covenant promise to be with his people and be their God. In verse 4 he is with the Spirit as the Comforter who wipes away our tears. In verse 5 he is with the Father as the re-creator, making all things new. In verse 6 he is the Alpha and the Omega, the beginning and the end, the eternal, everlasting, and almighty God. He is the root and the shoot of David (22:16). He is the free and living water (21:6) who satisfies our thirsty souls. He is the Lamb (22:1), the light (22:5), the lamp (21:23)—indeed, the very life of the city. Everything that is bright and beautiful in the everlasting city of God shines with the radiant glory of our Savior Jesus Christ, who is the most beautiful one to see in the most beautiful place we can imagine.

Dust to Glory

The risen Lord Jesus Christ, glorified bodily in his incarnation, will be the focus of our worship. Thus the dust of earth will sit on the throne of heaven. Here is how the Scottish theologian Thomas Boston described his glorious appearance:

> [The saints] shall see Jesus Christ, God and man, with their bodily eyes, as He will never lay aside the human nature. They will behold that glorious blessed body, which is personally united to the divine nature, and exalted above principalities and powers and every name that is named. There we shall see, with our eyes, that very body which was born of Mary at Bethlehem, and cruci-

fied at Jerusalem between two thieves: the blessed head that was crowned with thorns; the face that was spit upon; the hands and feet that were nailed to the cross; all shining with inconceivable glory. The glory of the man Christ will attract the eyes of all the saints.[7]

Boston also said this: "Who can conceive the happiness of the saints in the presence chamber of the great King, where he sits in his chair of state, making his glory eminently to appear in the man Christ?"[8]

Jonathan Edwards spoke in a similar vein at the funeral of his dear friend David Brainerd, the pioneer missionary to the Native Americans of eastern Pennsylvania. Brainerd had been blessed to see more than one hundred people come to faith in Jesus Christ through his ministry. Yet at the tender age of twenty-nine, he contracted a fatal disease and died in the Edwards's home. Edwards was grief-stricken over the death of his friend and the loss of a gifted missionary, as is evident from his words at the funeral. Reflecting on the human frailty of our earthly tabernacle, which will soon decay and fall, Edwards said:

O, how infinitely great will be the privilege and happiness of those, who, at that time shall go to be with Christ in his glory . . . where he sits on the throne, as the King of angels, and the God of the universe; shining forth as the Sun of that world of glory; . . . there most freely and intimately to converse with him, and fully to enjoy his love, as his friends and brethren; there to share with him in the infinite pleasure and joy which he has in the enjoyment of his Father—there to sit with him on his throne, to reign with him in the possession of all things . . . and to join with him in joyful songs of praise to his Father and our Father, to his God and our God forever and ever![9]

7. Thomas Boston, *Human Nature in Its Fourfold State* (Edinburgh: Banner of Truth, 1989), 452–53.

8. Ibid., 450.

9. Jonathan Edwards, *Jonathan Edwards: Representative Selections*, ed. Clarence H. Faust and Thomas H. Johnson (New York: Hill and Wang, 1935), 173–74.

WE'VE ONLY JUST BEGUN

The final thing to say is that when creation is recapitulated—when the curse is reversed, salvation is consummated, and Christ is enthroned—then glory will only have just begun. The new heaven and the new earth will be everything that Revelation promises, and infinitely more—*forever*. The sufferings of persecution will last only a little while, but the triumph of our reign will last forever.

Eternity is essential to the blessedness of the new heaven and the new earth. If they did not last forever, then they could not captivate us with their blessing. But the repeated promise of Revelation is that all of these things will be ours forever.

When I was a young child, the everlasting nature of eternity filled me with a kind of dread. The theological question that got me up out of bed at night to go down and talk to my parents more than any other was the awesomeness of infinity. Yet when we come to the end of the book of Revelation, we see clearly that the eternality of heaven is essential to the blessedness of the people of God.

One of the biggest frustrations we have with life in this fallen world is that "all good things must come to an end." It is not just the bad things in life that disappoint us, but also the end of all the good things. Sometimes it happens right in the middle of our happiness: as we are enjoying some sweet experience, suddenly we have the realization that it's going to leave us, that it's going to pass away, that we can't hold on to it. We wish we could, but we can't.

The people of God in glory will not know this bittersweet feeling because when we get to heaven, the blessings of God will be ours forever and ever, uninterrupted for all eternity.

I still remember the intense sadness I felt the summer of 1977, when I was only ten years old. We had spent the summer in England studying literature with students from Wheaton College. It was one of the best summers ever: castles and cathedrals, soccer and Frisbee, singing and worship, lectures and books, friendships to last a lifetime. At the end of the summer several students gave a farewell concert. They closed with a song by Seals and Crofts: "We May Never Pass This Way (Again)." As they sang, a deep melancholy settled over the room.

Afterward, the lead singer said, "We never should have ended the concert that way." Maybe he was right. I will never forget the sadness I felt that night. The summer was passing. Something was leaving us that could never be recovered. None of us would ever pass that way again.

The same is true of all our earthly pleasures. The holidays pass. Vacation comes to an end. The party is over. The time comes to retire from a job you love or to stop playing a sport you enjoy. Friends and family move away. Children go off to college. Sooner or later, we have to say good-bye to everything in life, including the people we love the most in the world. It is all passing away.

THE LAST HEAVEN AND THE LAST EARTH

But when the glory comes, nothing will ever pass away again. The Scripture says that "the world is passing away along with its desires, but whoever does the will of God abides forever" (1 John 2:17). The *new* heaven and the *new* earth will be the *last* heaven and the *last* earth. They will remain in the brightness of their glory forever. This is why they are described in terms of gold and jewels—precious things from earth that point to the permanence of heaven.

The brightness of that glory will be the radiant splendor of God himself. Since *his* glory will never fade, *our* glory will never be diminished. It truly will be an eternal glory—glory in absolute perfection extended out into eternity—a forever of "forevers"—a joy that will never, ever end.

Here is how C. S. Lewis tried to express the timeless joy of eternal life at the end of his book *The Last Battle*:

> The things that began to happen after that were so great and beautiful that I cannot write them. And for us this is the end of all

the stories, and we can most truly say that they all lived happily ever after. But for them it was only the beginning of the real story. All their life in this world had only been the cover and the title page: now at last they were beginning Chapter One of the Great Story which no one on earth has read: which goes on for ever: in which every chapter is better than the one before.[10]

Everyone who looks forward to the new heaven and the new earth may pray in hope the way John Donne prayed. As the great English preacher and poet looked ahead to the infinite worship of God, he lifted up this beautiful prayer:

> Bring us, O Lord, at our last awakening into the house and gate of heaven, to enter into that gate and dwell in that house, where there shall be no darkness nor dazzling, but one equal light; no noise nor silence, but one equal music; no fears nor hopes, but one equal possession; no ends nor beginning, but one equal eternity; in the habitation of thy glory and dominion, world without end.[11]

John the Evangelist offered a simpler prayer. At the end of Revelation, he quoted the last words of Christ that are recorded in Scripture, "Surely I am coming soon." And when he heard these words, John cried out, "Amen. Come, Lord Jesus!" (Rev. 22:20).

This is our prayer as well: "Come, Lord Jesus!" And when we make this prayer, we stand under the benediction that John pronounced on everyone who lives in hope for the day when all things will be made new: "The grace of the Lord Jesus be with all. Amen" (22:21).

10. C. S. Lewis, *The Last Battle* (New York: Macmillan, 1956), 165.
11. John Donne, quoted in John Polkinghorne, *The God of Hope and the End of the World* (New Haven, CT: Yale University Press, 2002), 98.

Appendix

BIBLICAL FOUNDATIONS FOR SEEKING GOD'S JUSTICE IN A SINFUL WORLD

A Panel Discussion

THABITI ANYABWILE, VODDIE BAUCHAM JR.,
D. A. CARSON, TIMOTHY KELLER,
MIGUEL NÚÑEZ, AND JOHN PIPER

The years 2014 and 2015 will long be remembered in America for outbreaks of racial violence in several cities, including Ferguson, Missouri, and New York City. Issues of justice for minorities returned to the headlines and forced evangelicals back to Scripture to think and rethink what it means for justice to be served in a society. How should a pastor or a church respond to the violence and division that continue to roil our country and, by extension, the body of Christ? How should Christians respond when things go terribly wrong between law enforcement and sectors of the public it is called to protect? What does Scripture say about justice? How should we apply its timeless wisdom to our lives, and how should we teach it in our congregations?

These are but a few of the crucial questions that punctuated the informal conversation that took place between six participants in TGC's 2015 National Conference. We have edited the conversation only slightly to capture the real-time engagement of real-world issues between a group of men who are deeply invested in the life of the local church. So here we present that conversation to you, praying that it will help shed needed light on what has become a major question that demands thoughtful, careful, biblical answers among evangelicals today.

Jeff Robinson Sr.

Don Carson: Unless you were living utterly cut off from all news sources in the digital world during the past few months, you have to be aware of the very significant discussion that has taken place in the wake, especially, of Ferguson, New York City, and more recent events as well. It is important that we talk about these things—not least when we disagree in our perceptions of some of them. Merely throwing brickbats and yelling at each other is not going to help. As Christians we want to talk about these things with minds profoundly submitted to Scripture and eager to be reformed by the Word of God, not least when our emotions are so heavily involved. . . .

On this panel, we want to paint on a broad canvas. That is to say, we want to think about justice issues—not just racial issues. There are a lot of other justice issues apart from the racial ones: poverty, consumerism, the white slave trade, many other things that could be mentioned, corruption in politics—any number of justice issues that really need a foundational way of thinking. So we're going to try to talk about some of these things at a biblical, theological level with clear implications and applications to some of the issues. We won't agree on everything, but our aim is to submit everything to Scripture as best we can, with love for one another and a deep, deep desire to bow to the lordship of Christ.

The first question is What are the biblical texts and theological themes that should most control our thinking about justice and righteousness issues in our lives, in the church, in the time and place in the world where God has placed us?

Tim Keller: It's intriguing that in Genesis 9—because all human beings are made in the image of God—God even holds animals responsible for killing a human being. Because a human being is made in the image of God, he says, I will require the blood even of animals. It's also intriguing that James says you should not speak abusively; you shouldn't curse people who are made in the image of God. So James forbids even speaking harshly to someone made in the image of God. The *imago Dei* is foundational, I think, for talking about how you treat people. If even cursing somebody is wrong because he or she is made in the image of God, or if even animals are held responsible in some way—I've not quite figured out how God does that—it doesn't surprise me that in the beginning of Amos, chapters 1 and 2, God holds the pagan nations around Israel responsible for genocide, for imperialism, and for oppression and cruelty. These are pagan nations; they do not have the law of God, they do not have the Bible, but it's very clear that God still holds them responsible for justice, for treating human beings with justice as beings made in the image of God. So you can see the basis of what we would consider caring about people's rights, giving people what they deserve, treating all human beings as having infinite dignity in texts like that.

Voddie Baucham: When I try to think about these things from an overarching philosophical perspective that roots and grounds us in why it is that people should be treated a certain way, we begin with God and what it means to be created *imago Dei*. But then I go to the second table of the law to understand how that's manifested, which is what I think Paul does in Romans 14 with "owe no one anything, except to love." And then, what does he do? He enumerates the second table of the law. I do think we need to have this philosophical overarching understanding of people having inherent dignity and value because of the image of God. But then when we sort of put feet on it and talk specifically about what would be right and what would be wrong in the treatment of people, we have to come to the moral law; we have to come to that transcendent moral code that God has given us and to which we are all held accountable.

Thabiti Anyabwile: I like where these brothers have started. In the beginning, and just prior to the *imago Dei* creation, we're told that God wants us to fill the earth, to multiply; and in part that's to bring forth his glory. Malachi 2:15 tells us why he established marriage—that he might have offspring that would bring him glory. So questions of justice are connected with questions of worship too. Our proper relationship to God and our filling of the earth with his glory has something to do with human flourishing and how we treat others as image bearers who themselves have been created to reflect the glory of God. I'm with these brothers in starting at the beginning because I think a foundation is laid there for thinking about justice and its outworking today.

John Piper: I would go up a level. . . . The person in the universe who has rights is God. He has rights. Justice is acting in a way so that God gets his rights. That is the most fundamental meaning of justice. God acts according to his rights. And if you say, "What are God's rights?" any behavior that accords with the infinite value of God is a right behavior. So ultimate rightness is behaviors, thoughts, feelings that are conformed to the infinite value of God. If we start with man, even with the *imago Dei*, without saying that first, we will probably go skewed eventually in a manward direction, in a man-centered world. I know Tim, who started the way he did, will be the one who most effectively relates the gospel to this issue by saying the gospel deals with making sure God gets his rights in punishing those who've offended him on the cross, so there can be mercy. The gospel will make no sense eventually if we haven't started with the righteousness of God, which includes

God's right to punish those who don't act in accord with his infinite value.

DC: Tim, do you agree with him on that?

TK: Yes. He is correct.

DC: Miguel, do you want to correct these brothers?

Miguel Núñez: I just want to add a couple of things. I see the character of God—the God who is just and righteous, who gave us a law that is also just. But all that is unjust began because that law was violated. The image of God was corrupted when the law of God was violated. Anything I see that is imperfect or unjust today is the result of that fall. And God is redeeming his image in mankind. When you think about loving God with all your heart, soul, mind, and strength, if you love God, you should be loving everything that he loves. We know from the Bible that God loves justice; that's part of what he is. And secondly, the Bible calls us to love our neighbor as ourselves and to treat that neighbor the way we would like to be treated. So I think any degree of injustice is the result of violating that law and corrupting that image. All the texts dealing with such themes are foundational to these issues.

DC: Let's pursue that one a bit further before we come into the next range of questions. How many of these foundational issues are preached in our churches and well understood in our churches? By "our churches," I primarily mean the churches and denominations we represent, including TGC-related churches. Has there been a failure to get across some of these foundational issues—lifting up the centrality of God and its entailments?

VB: I would say yes, there's been massive failure in this regard. Man-centeredness is the order of the day. One of the reasons there are so many people who are so attracted to what's happening at things like the Gospel Coalition is this revival of God-centered thinking and the rightness of God-centered thinking. The Lord's sheep know his voice, and when people hear God being magnified and glorified and God at the center and the gospel of God at the center, people are attracted to that. And one of the reasons it's so attractive is people have been starved of it.

DC: Let me come to a second question. It's a tier down in some ways. What are some of the reasons that devout Christians who believe the Bible and really think that they are bowing to Christ's lordship can nevertheless disagree on an array of justice social issues as strongly as they do? What are the reasons?

TK: One reason is different experience. If you are white, if you are black, you're just going to have a different daily experience. And I think it's normal for us to universalize—the way we see things is the way it is. That's not the only answer to your question. But some people have had a more privileged experience; some people have had less privileged experiences. That's one of the reasons.

VB: Our theology also goes into this—because there's a reason that, for example, Tim's wrong on baptism and I'm not. Kidding aside, in all seriousness I use that as an illustration of how people can very much love one another and can very much be eye to eye on so many things, but because of different theological presuppositions and the different things we bring to our understanding of the text of Scripture, they lead us in different directions. One of the problems we have is that we don't allow for that in these discussions. If we're talking about issues like baptism, and we see someone over here who's going in this direction on baptism and someone over here who's going in that direction on baptism, we acknowledge the theological divergence. We don't say that one of them is a good person and the other deserves to be beaten. But on a particularly visceral issue, all of a sudden we say one person is unjust and the other is just, when what we're seeing is a manifestation of the same truth.

TA: In some ways, your last question is connected with the previous question, and so you're trying to get us to mix it up a bit here, and that's good. I agree with these brothers, and I guess what I'd want to say is, certainly along with what they have said, I think it is true that when it comes to thinking through what the Bible says about justice from God all the way down, to the ethic to love—and I'm going to risk overgeneralizing—I don't think most Christians have ever been discipled in this area.

What these brothers just did when you asked your first question was just sort of reaching into the Scripture and bringing out the second table of the law, or reaching into the Scripture and reflecting on the *imago Dei*, or reaching up a level higher and thinking about the rights that God has and bringing it down to justice. Yet if we were to poll the room, my guess is the majority of persons in here would say, "Nobody's ever taught me to work through these subjects so deeply and so quickly, either to come up with solid answers on a panel like this one, or, more importantly, in the face of an actual conflict that rushes to the fore and shapes what I'm thinking and what I'm doing."

I don't think the American church is very well discipled to think through justice writ large or justice in particular situations. And most of our discipleship has come through whatever political influences we have had or whatever personal influences we have had, and so, we're not in the first instance reflecting deeply on the Scriptures. If we were, we'd still have different starting points sometimes and places where we'd go different ways, but we'd at least be having the same conversation about what the Book says. Often we're not having the same conversation.

TK: I want to build on what Thabiti just said. There's no doubt that we are listening to political voices and not thinking theologically about the subject. For example, right now I would say the basic liberal political understanding of justice is that the individual needs to be protected from the society. The individual has to be free to live any way he or she wants to live no matter what society or family or religion says. The conservative understanding of justice is actually that the individual has to be protected from the state, from the government, from regulation, from the law. They are very different and they are both too thin, biblically speaking. They both resonate with certain aspects of a biblical understanding of justice, but if all you do is read the liberal websites or the conservative websites and you are just completely immersed in them, and then suddenly as a Christian you come to the Ferguson issue or the Staten Island issue, instead of really thinking it out in a biblically proactive way, you are really just following the crowd, your particular political crowd and not thinking theologically. You can definitely see it in the comments section on TGC's website. You can see where people got their ideas; they usually don't come from the Scriptures.

MN: The more I get to know people, the more I realize how important worldviews are. Part of the problem is that worldviews are not just related to knowledge. We can get a lot of knowledge from the Bible. But worldviews are related to emotions, to experiences in life, family upbringing. In dealing with people and in counseling, even with the people in my own congregation, I realize that, after hearing the truth and knowing the truth—the knowledge, the intellectual aspect of it—people are still behaving in a different way than what I've been preaching to them. So I think we need to be aware of the worldviews of the audience to whom we are preaching and try to preach the truth of the Bible addressing the worldviews of the audience we have in front of us. That's why having a good idea of who is in your congregation is very important, because the way Latin Americans look at life is not necessarily the same way North Americans look at life, even when they are believers and even when they might be equally sanctified. And speaking of sanctification, sometimes I think it's just that—the degree of sanctification is different between one person and another.

DC: Why don't you just take a minute and tell us some ways that Latin Americans on the whole look at the world differently from North Americans? It would be good for us to hear that.

MN: I'll just use some very simple, everyday experiences. Latin Americans, in general, are not on time! We're always late. From the North American point of view, that is very selfish. . . . But we don't see that as anything selfish because it is part of the culture. . . . My wife is from New York and she taught me that. She'd call me for dinner, and I'd be ten or fifteen minutes late, and I didn't think that was a big deal. But for her, who had cooked and had put the dinner on the table—and it was warm—it was kind of selfish that I didn't come when she told me that dinner was ready. That's just one aspect of it.

I could go on and on and give you many examples. Certainly, life is very different. We are not as organized as the Anglo mind is, and that is not a problem for many of us. Traffic is very chaotic in many of our cities, and we don't see anything wrong with it. You go there and you get crazy at the lack of organization, yet you see that the Latin Americans are very much at peace with each other in even joking around about those issues. So you grow up there and, for you, that's normal.

You could apply such different stances to racism, level of income, education, and on and on and on, but I think worldviews constitute one of the hardest things to destroy from people's minds. So preaching to create a biblical worldview, one that is not just based on knowledge, but on how you should act as a result your knowledge, is paramount, and I think that's where applications may vary from culture to culture. The truth that you are expounding is the same no matter where you are; the application may have different colors. I think that's important.

DC: As I recall the passage in James 1, James tells us that rich believers must recognize that they are like flowers in the field that die and pass away, so they should learn humility, whereas the poor need to learn of their high position in Christ. In other words, the same gospel is applied in very different ways to the two groups. That means that pastors, likewise, have to be sensitive to the different blind spots of the different persons in the congregation, especially when it's a really diverse congregation. The task becomes very challenging. So what are some of the things you, collectively, think we're discerning poorly, we're not thinking through carefully, in terms of how to apply the Word of God to the way people think and act on a broad front of justice issues?

JP: I wanted to follow up on the previous question, which was "Why are there all the differences?" and it came around to, we haven't been well discipled. If that's true—if the people haven't been well discipled or the pastors haven't done it well—why haven't we done it well? My encouragement would be, I'm hindered from tackling some things because I don't have the answers at the street level. It's easy for me to talk theory. I say, "What about this and this and this and this? I'm not sure what I think, and therefore, I'm not even inclined to go to the theoretical level; let's just talk about something I know." And so, my guess is, one reason pastors don't take up justice issues is they're not really sure what to say at a certain level, and my encouragement would be take it as far as you can take it.

A lot of the Bible is clear on this. You could preach a whole message on Tim's first point on the *imago Dei* from Genesis 9 and James where you don't curse people made in the image of God—that's important to hear. My suggestion is, don't fail to disciple your people at the levels that you can. That's one reason we have been silent. The other is cowardice—we haven't done it because we are afraid to do it. There are going to be people in our church who don't like what we are going to say, and therefore we're scared to say it. Those are two motives for what you're saying is true, namely, that we haven't done as good a job as we could.

VB: What I would add to that is, going back to the worldview issue, there is always this sense that we've bought into this idea that experience trumps all, and therefore if I don't have the experience, then I can't even speak the truth I know because the truth of Scripture is not as powerful as people's experiences. And because we have sort of bought into that false way of thinking, I think that there are a lot of people who are afraid of this idea that we will speak something that is true scripturally, somebody will feel like we've been insensitive to their circumstance and experience—which trumps anything that we could possibly have said because, after all, God's knowledge is not nearly as significant as the knowledge of the person who is experiencing something on the ground—and so we just sort of step back in that fear.

I think we need to deal with that first, within ourselves, and secondly, I think we need to help people understand that our individual experience doesn't trump anything; our experience has to be brought into subjection in the same way that we are to take every thought captive to obedience to Christ. So I think we our doing ourselves and we are doing our people a disservice when we assume because we haven't had their experience, we don't have anything to contribute on some particular issue. We don't want to be arrogant and pretend that experience doesn't matter at all, but we also don't want to commit the opposite error, which is acting as if it's the only thing that matters.

TK: To Don's question about the justice-related issues we're not talking about, in the very beginning of my ministry, I preached through the book of Amos, using Alec Motyer's little book in The Bible Speaks Today series. It was very striking how the book talked about the fact that, in general, poor people have more trouble getting justice than wealthy people; they're not treated fairly. Some societies are better than others at this, of course, but the simple fact of the matter is that in our society, this is the case too. Basically, if you don't have money, you don't get equal treatment. Bill Stuntz's book *The Collapse of American Criminal Justice*—he was the leading authority on criminal justice—said very clearly, in the main takeaway of the book, that if you don't have money, you don't get justice. Race is a big problem too, because very often race and economics are tied together. Basically, however, he demonstrates that the less money you have, the less likely you are to get a fair shake in the American criminal justice system. He makes a strong case, and I think it pretty much proves it.

What do you do about that? The challenge is massive. Actually, I would say that is a valid application of preaching on the book of Amos, because there is constant discussions about that—about the poor being treated fairly, being given the same hearing in the court as the rich. And to say there has never been a society like that, and ours isn't like that either—to say there's never been a society that recognized that because of sin we ought to realize that the poor in our community, unless they get a lot of help, unless the kids that are born into those poor families get a lot of help, they're not going to get a fair shake—is a necessary first step. They didn't choose to be born where they were born. Children born into my family versus children born into a poor community in the same town have a three hundred times better chance of staying out of jail. So it seems to me when you're preaching, you can make those kinds of applications without directly saying, "Therefore, vote for this candidate" or "This law is wrong" or anything like that. I do think we are afraid to apply the truth even at that level in our preaching, and we shouldn't be afraid to do that.

TA: The things we are missing in this conversation are the things that are not on the news outlets we are watching. They're the things that are not in the time lines on our Twitter feeds if our Twitter feeds are mainly comprised of people like us in our camp. They're the things that other people write about that we don't think about because we are preoccupied with certain sets of issues. In order to not miss things, I think we have to have wider exposure. And we have to afford to people the same kind of generosity with their differing perspectives that we would want as we engage those kinds of circles.

In a lot of conversations right now, when you raise the justice issue, the word *justice* is almost ceded over to the left as a liberal idea. That's a good Bible word. The Bible has a lot to say about that. And words like *liberal* and *conservative* become sort of the imprimatur of who's trustworthy and who's not. . . . In humility, I think we miss a lot of issues because our pastors don't preach about them, we're not naturally inclined to read about them, our natural networks become kinds of cul-de-sacs in which we huddle up with people who think more or less like us, and we rob ourselves of a richer understanding that could be ours with more liberal reading.

What are some of those issues? Well, we talked here about criminal justice and mass incarceration. We can talk about poverty and issues related to poverty. We can talk about things like education funding and how that gets done and whether education dollars are distributed in ways that are just. We can talk about sex trafficking. There's a whole range of things. Sometimes it's like we fail to remember that we live in an unjust world. We're surrounded by injustice. And what we need are open eyes and open hearts to see more and feel more for the things that we begin to discover as we sort of move out of what's comfortable for us.

VB: I think one of the issues we have largely ignored—and this is something I have just become more and more aware of—we have been in war for almost a decade and a half; people made in the image of God dying almost every day for the last decade and a half, and we don't even think about war. It's not one of the issues we even raise—every day, people in the image of God dying for the last decade and a half, and we're talking about expanding our war efforts and there is no end in sight to our war efforts. And as Christians, one of the deafening silences out there is—I'm not talking Vietnam-era hate the troops and all that sort of stuff—I'm talking about every once in a while saying, "Can you tell us when we're going to end this? Can you tell us why we're doing this? Can you tell us what we're going to accomplish?" I think the fact that we don't talk about that when people for the last decade and a half have been dying and killing almost every day—to me, that's deafening silence.

TA: That's a good example of the importance of having folks who are your conversation partners who aren't in your circle. I'm strongly resonating with what he's saying, and I'm thinking, I have a lot of friends who are on the so-called left who have been talking about that a lot for a long time, for a decade and a half, raising questions about the justice of these wars from the beginning, but he's absolutely right, if those folks are not in your circle, that's a huge blind spot.

VB: But even those folks are usually not talking about it from the perspective of the image of God. They may be talking about it from the standpoint of power and imperialism and these sorts of things, but I'm talking about from a biblical, people-made-in-the-image-of-God perspective.

TA: That's why we have to have discipleship. That's why we have to have this sort of basic theological orientation, so that even as we are reading our Bibles with people who don't share our presuppositions, we can have that conversation without losing our moorings.

JP: Just so we don't sound too dovish up here, I think we ought to take out Boko Haram—it's overdue. When I say we, I don't mean the Christian church. . . . I'm not personally into war, I hate that kind of thing. But when Boko Haram gets away with barbarous cruelty over and over and over, I think Romans 13 exists for something and that the police in the country and the military at the national level carry the sword not in vain. There are certain kinds of wretched behavior that ought to be reacted to with pretty swift violence.

VB: Since we're talking about justice, would you say then that America is unjust for not going into another country and dealing with an injustice there, or would you say that those countries are being unjust because they are the ones responsible according to Romans 13, within their jurisdiction, and have not addressed the issue?

JP: This is why I don't preach on this issue, because I'm not sure. This is a perfect illustration of what I'm talking about: somebody's going to walk up to you after you say what you say and ask you that question and you say, "Well, I'm not preaching on that again! I'm not preaching on war again. I don't have a clue." My guess is the answer is both—and the latter more so than the former. The farther you are away from something, probably, the less responsible you are. I base that on the parable of the good Samaritan. He's responsible because the guy is there on the side of the road. If he's on the other side of the country, he's not responsible for that guy on the side of the road. He doesn't know about it. The more we know, the more opportunity we have, and the more capability we have, and the more we care, then our responsibility jacks up, and so I don't really know whether America should police the world. I don't know.

TA: Brother, to your credit, you've been talking about justice issues for pretty much the life of your ministry, and unpopular justice issues with regularity in your church. Here's why I think it's an important question, and here's why I'm glad he asked it. . . . The proximity argument for me is limited in response to that kind of question and here's why: I think if we fall too easily onto proximity, we fall too easily into complacency. There are things we ought to know about. There are things we ought to be learning about. There are things we ought to be engaging if in fact we are going to bear credible witness where we live and in increasingly wider circles, right? That's not to argue that we have responsibility on an individual level to posse up and go fix Boko Haram, but we do have a responsibility on an individual level if we are going to love our neighbors and love our enemies, to know something about them, to know something about the world and have a posture that leans into these sets of issues.

I would answer yes to both of your [Voddie Baucham's] questions—Is it a justice issue and does the United States have some responsibility with regard to Boko Haram, or is it a matter of, inside a government and a country, it only gets policed there? I would argue yes, with the second being more obviously yes, but I want to argue the first one yes as well. This country's foreign policy toward Africa has been atrocious—from participation in the slave trade, all the way down to its silence on apartheid, coming all the way forward to how it has dealt with famine. The one exception to that, ironically, is Bush, who had a pretty good policy with regard to AIDs and things of that sort in Africa. But otherwise, it's been atrocious. Meanwhile, a president like Clinton could go and mediate in the troubles in Ireland, for example, or we could adopt some posture of intervention with regard to Bosnia-Herzegovina.

This is no less a justice issue in Africa; it should have parity. We want to grow more and more to be impartial in our concern about these things, and we need to advocate that in our government, so I think it is a justice issue for us to face. And then I'm slowing down because I don't know all the solutions on the ground. But at least at that point, I'm going, "Yeah, and it's a justice issue in Nigeria and its government and its false application of the sword"—so within the country as well.

VB: This is one of those areas where there is brotherly disagreement, because I would argue that, as Americans, our government officials have a jurisdiction to which they are limited, and that jurisdiction is the protection of our country and our borders. It is not the job of America to go and police the world. Once you start down that road, what you do is a number of things: First, you disrespect the sovereignty of other nations around the world. That's one of the problems we have in America: the sphere sovereignty of the government is overstepping its bounds into the sphere sovereignty of the family, and the sphere sovereignty of the church, and the sphere sovereignty of other nations, and so on and so forth. The other issue is, how do we determine the level at which injustice has to exist somewhere else in the world before we then go in and say, "We're crossing your borders to make you just"? From my perspective, that's dangerous, and I don't want to give any government the right to cross another government's borders to make them just.

TA: I'm glad for this conversation, because it gets to model how friends differ. And I'm glad to say publicly that Voddie and I are friends. We have ministered together in the gospel. We have served together, we've traveled together, in case someone has mistaken our different views to mean that we are somehow feuding. This is my dear brother in the Lord, and I love having these conversations with him because he's honest. To your question, I think if we take an isolationist, protectionist policy, it's ultimately going to be self-defeating. I think the history of diplomacy has proven that. So there's some sense in which, for the public good, the country has to take an interest in international affairs and to engage that.

VB: I never said we didn't. I'm a noninterventionist, not an isolationist.

TA: So where we begin to track apart is this question of intervention. You've already given one answer to that question in your comments, and that is where the actions of another country infringe upon the welfare and benefits of American citizens, so we're completely agreed on that. I want to add some categories to that. One category I think we want to add is genocide. We're back then, as Christians, to thinking about people being made in the image of God, the value of life being incalculable. When human life is being taken at a vast scale, the loving thing to do is to intervene and stop the slaughter. I love the way Dr. King defines justice; he said in his 1955 Montgomery bus boycott speech, "Justice is love correcting everything that revolts against love." So the loving thing to do is to intervene on behalf of those persons who are being slaughtered by their own government; it would be unjust to stand aside and watch that happen. I would argue that is grounds for intervention.

VB: I think there is a categorical error here—there's an excluded middle. There's a fallacy in your argument because the assumption is we either watch it happen or we send the most powerful military in the world across other people's borders. There are a lot of steps in between.

TA: I absolutely agree. You are making explicit something I was assuming. A lot of diplomacy happens.

VB: And helping neighbors to do that as well, right? So we look at, for example, ISIS, and everybody's saying, "We've got to go get ISIS," and "Why aren't we getting ISIS?" My question is: Turkey has a half-million man army. Why aren't they going to get ISIS? That middle is where the work has got to be done.

TA: Amen. I'm with you on that.

DC: Can I stick my nose in here so one or two others can get involved in the conversation? For our last few minutes, I want to turn our discussion in a different direction. This has been useful. It's important to hear Christians who take Scripture seriously trying to think things through from fundamental principles and get at least some meeting of minds on some of these issues. Confession is good for the soul; I have a son in the military, so I've tried to think about these things quite a bit, but matters of just war theory are not easy, and if the only alternative is pacifism, it seems to me you're stepping away from a fair bit of Scripture; but that doesn't mean any of it is easy.

How do such issues of justice, as important as they are, as heated as these topics are in many of our circles, how are they tied to a rich, thick understanding of the gospel? How should they be tied to the fundamentals of the gospel at the heart of our preaching of Jesus Christ and him crucified?

TA: My mind goes pretty quickly to Romans 3:21–26. I think it was Leon Morris who called it the most important paragraph in the Bible, where Paul asserts that God left some sins unpunished until Christ. And in the gospel, in the crucifixion of the Lord Jesus Christ, and in the resurrection, God shows himself to be just and the justifier of those who trust in him. That means a couple of things: one, that whatever injustices we talk about in the world, they are in fact either accounted for in God's wrath on the unrepentant or accounted for in the punishment of his Son as a substitute for sinners. It also means a second thing: that all these justice issues that we talk about that live far off, they come home most pressingly in terms of our personal sin, our personal accountability, and our personal failure to give to God what is his right. So the justice issue that we most have to be concerned about individually is our own sin before God—robbing him of glory and obedience that he is due. And either we will give an account for that in his judgment or we will escape in his mercy through our faith in Christ, who has given himself as a sacrifice for sin.

MN: The gospel is the message that can change the heart and the mind of a person. Unless that takes place, I don't think anything is going to change. Education doesn't have that power. Technology doesn't have that power. We saw that after the First World War.

The humanists got together and they thought we learned the hard way, so we would never see this again, but a few years later we had the Second World War.

The gospel is the only hope for mankind, so I think it is directly related to issues of injustice of any kind, of any nature, of any level. Without it, there is no hope. That's why I think we need to keep preaching the gospel, to change people's minds and hearts. But we need to challenge these believers, so that when they go out into society, they will know what it means to be the salt and the light in the world. That's one of the problems: we have taught people the gospel and how you get born again, but we have not taught enough about how you live that gospel as a physician, an engineer, a plumber, a painter. So I think there is a direct correlation between one and the other.

TK: The gospel, meaning propitiation through substitution, refuses to pit holiness and judgment against love and mercy. On the cross, both of those brilliantly coincide and shine forth. I do sense that most political theory, whether it has to do with foreign policy or with criminal justice, veers either toward the antinomian or toward the moralistic and legalistic. And if you really have an understanding of the gospel and say, "We're not going to choose between those things," it gets more difficult, frankly. But what I thought was really instructive about this panel was that there is good theological grounding for what everybody was saying up here, and that's the reason why you cannot become, as a Christian, purely dovish or purely hawkish. You can't just get relativistic and say, "Look, everybody's got to be free to live the way they want," or become moralistic and overdo virtue and ethics or overdo individualism. I really do think the gospel forces us to come together as a community and honor all the different aspects of God's attributes, and honor all the different aspects of theology and not just reduce and oversimplify them. That's what I think almost all political parties tend to do right now.

VB: And the gospel is the only thing that explains why it matters. It's the only thing that explains it adequately because Christ died for a people. We have the adoption as sons. And so, now, because of the gospel, I have the ability to look outside myself and see the *imago Dei* in other people, and see the fullness of the reward for which Christ died, and see how significant that reward is to him and how that makes those people significant to me; and that's when I begin to think about this from a right perspective. It's no longer an exercise of power. It's no longer an exercise of even appeasing my own conscience. It becomes an exercise of me acknowledging the reality of our oneness in Christ and acknowledging that I have a vested interest in you as another member of the body of Christ because I desire for the body to be nurtured and treated properly. The gospel is the only thing that gives us that.

JP: The gospel unleashes in the world a commitment not to live for justice, but to live for more than justice. Justice is minimalist. A life devoted to treating people as they deserve is not a Christian life. God, in the gospel, treated us better than we deserve. That's not justice—we don't get justice in the gospel. God got justice in the gospel. We don't get justice in the gospel, we get grace. And he unleashes on the world a people in churches, and spilling over out of churches, who treat each other way beyond justice. You shouldn't walk through the day or through your life thinking, "How can I be just?" You should walk through the world thinking, "How can I be gracious? How can I be loving? How can I be kind? How can I love my enemy? How can I go the extra mile? How can I, when I am sued, give him my cloak as well?" The gospel unleashes something way beyond justice, so Christians shouldn't be known mainly as the justice people. That's minimalist; you start there and go beyond. So Christ will be known in the culture when we treat people better than they deserve, not as they deserve.

CONTRIBUTORS

Thabiti Anyabwile (MS, North Carolina State University) is a pastor at Anacostia River Church in southeast Washington, DC. He is a council member of the Gospel Coalition.

Voddie Baucham Jr. (DMin, Southeastern Baptist Theological Seminary) is dean of the seminary at African Christian University in Lusaka, Zambia.

D. A. Carson (PhD, University of Cambridge) is research professor of New Testament at Trinity Evangelical Divinity School. He is a cofounder and president of the Gospel Coalition.

Mark Dever (PhD, University of Cambridge) is senior pastor of Capitol Hill Baptist Church in Washington, DC. He is a council member of the Gospel Coalition.

J. Ligon Duncan III (PhD, University of Edinburgh) is chancellor and CEO, as well as John E. Richards Professor of Systematic and Historical Theology, at Reformed Theological Seminary in Jackson, Mississippi. He is a council member of the Gospel Coalition.

Timothy Keller (DMin, Westminster Theological Seminary) is founder and senior pastor of Redeemer Presbyterian Church in New York City. He is a cofounder and vice president of the Gospel Coalition.

Augustus Nicodemus Lopes (PhD, Westminster Theological Seminary) is senior pastor of the Presbyterian Church of Goiânia, Goiás, and vice president of the Presbyterian Church of Brazil.

Miguel Núñez (DMin, The Southern Baptist Theological Seminary) is senior pastor of International Baptist Church and president of Wisdom and Integrity Ministries in Santo Domingo, Dominican Republic. He is a council member of the Gospel Coalition.

John Piper (DTheol, University of Munich) is founder and teacher of desiringGod.org and chancellor of Bethlehem College & Seminary. He is a council member of the Gospel Coalition.

Jeff Robinson Sr. (PhD, The Southern Baptist Theological Seminary) is senior editor for the Gospel Coalition and pastor of Christ Fellowship Church in Louisville, Kentucky.

Philip Graham Ryken (DPhil, University of Oxford) is the eighth president of Wheaton College. He is a council member of the Gospel Coalition.

GENERAL INDEX

injustice, 151, 153
intermediate state, 10, 68, 115
intervention, 155–56
ISIS, 125, 156
Israel
    remnant of, 33, 38
    restoration of, 38, 45–46, 55, 56
Israel (northern tribes), 50

Jerusalem. *See also* New Jerusalem
    curse on, 126
    destruction of, 44
    punishment of, 50–51
    rebuilding of, 60
Jesus Christ
    circumcision of, 24–25
    continues his work today, 74–75
    death of, 65, 66, 70, 74, 84, 100,
        157
    defeated death, 101–2
    enthronement of, 133–34
    and eschatology, 11
    farewell discourse of, 63–77
    as fulfillment of prophecy, 33
    glory of, 41–42
    as God, 65
    going to the Father, 68–69, 73
    as High Priest, 48
    as last Adam, 98–99, 125
    as living water, 132
    obedience of, 99–100, 101, 113
    resurrection of, 66–67, 70, 74,
        96, 106, 157
    and resurrection of widow's son,
        128
    return of, 9, 10, 66–67, 82,
        104–5
    reveals the Father, 70–72
    as shoot from stump of Jesse,
        39–40
    as temple, 60
    as the way to the Father's house,
        69
judgment, 53–54, 86, 90
justice, 139–59

justification, ended chattel slavery,
    116
just war theory, 157

Keller, Tim, 126
King, Martin Luther, 156
knowledge of God, 35

labor not in vain, 101–5
last heaven and last earth, 137
Latin Americans, 147
law of God, 143
Lewis, C. S., 124, 137–38
liberals and conservatives, on jus-
    tice, 146, 151
life after death, 9
literal short-term prophecy, 46–47
Lloyd-Jones, D. Martyn, 15–16
longing for God, 59
longing for home, 119–21
Longman, Tremper, III, 14–15
love, 76, 145
    for enemies, 154, 159
    for God, 143
Lundin, Roger, 128

man-centeredness, 142, 143
many rooms, in Father's house,
    65–66
marriage, 22, 126–27
Marshall, Stephen, 116–17
Marx, Karl, 75, 80
materialism, 81
millennium, 47, 76
missiology, 100–105
mobile throne chariot (Ezekiel), 55
Moody, D. L., 120
morality, 90
More, Thomas, 88
Morris, Leon, 157
motivational speaking, 18
Motyer, Alec, 149

nations
    coming to the Messiah, 33, 38
    healing of, 56, 132

SCRIPTURE INDEX

52 Questions
& Answers for
Your Heart
& Mind

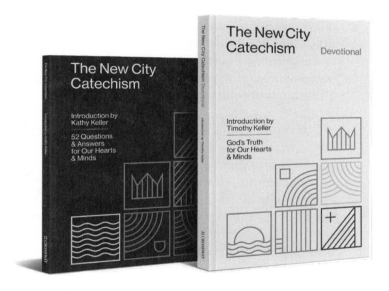

The New City Catechism is a gospel-centered resource that sets forth a summary of important Christian doctrine in the form of fifty-two questions and answers meant to be memorized and recited over the course of a year.

The New City Catechism Devotional features the same questions and answers as well as commentary written by leading contemporary and historical theologians that will help children and adults alike gain a deeper understanding of foundational Christian beliefs.

THE GOSPEL **COALITION**

The Gospel Coalition is a fellowship of evangelical churches deeply committed to renewing our faith in the gospel of Christ and to reforming our ministry practices to conform fully to the Scriptures. We have committed ourselves to invigorating churches with new hope and compelling joy based on the promises received by grace alone through faith alone in Christ alone.

We desire to champion the gospel with clarity, compassion, courage, and joy—gladly linking hearts with fellow believers across denominational, ethnic, and class lines. We yearn to work with all who, in addition to embracing our confession and theological vision for ministry, seek the lordship of Christ over the whole of life with unabashed hope in the power of the Holy Spirit to transform individuals, communities, and cultures.

Join the cause and visit TGC.org for fresh resources that will equip you to love God with all your heart, soul, mind, and strength, and to love your neighbor as yourself.

TGC.org